JONATHAN McKEE THE BULLYING BREAKTHROUGH

REAL HELP
FOR PARENTS
AND TEACHERS
OF THE BULLIED,
BYSTANDERS,
AND BULLIES

SHILOH RUN  PRESS
An Imprint of Barbour Publishing, Inc.

© 2018 by Jonathan McKee

Print ISBN 978-1-68322-688-8

eBook Editions:
Adobe Digital Edition (.epub) 978-1-68322-958-2
Kindle and MobiPocket Edition (.prc) 978-1-68322-961-2

Cover Design: Greg Jackson, Thinkpen Design

The author is represented by, and this book is published in association with, the literary agency of WordServe Literary Group, Ltd., www.wordserveliterary.com.

Published by Shiloh Run Press, an imprint of Barbour Publishing, Inc., 1810 Barbour Drive, Uhrichsville, Ohio 44683, www.shilohrunpress.com

Our mission is to inspire the world with the life-changing message of the Bible.

ecpa Member of the
Evangelical Christian
Publishers Association

Printed in the United States of America.

CONTENTS

ACKNOWLEDGMENTS

Thanks to God for sparing me from doing something irreversibly stupid when I was a kid to take out revenge on the group that targeted me. It's only by God's love and grace that I've been able to heal as much as I have. I rely on Him daily on this continued journey.

Thanks, Kelly—this book is because of you. Kelly is my publisher and friend who has partnered with me on countless projects now. This book only happened because she approached me after reading my cyberbullying chapter in *The Teen's Guide to Social Media and Mobile Devices* and talked me into writing a book to parents on the subject. You've come to me with two ideas now. . .and the first one is my bestseller. I guess we'll see with this one!

Thanks to my family for putting up with my insecurity and insensitivity. Lori, you're amazing! All those old bullies are so jealous. I married a cheerleader! (There's hope, fellow nerds!) If only they knew you are so much more. And Alec, Alyssa, and Ashley, I love you more than any words in the front of a book could ever express.

Thanks to so many friends who provided good counsel and ideas for this book. Daniel Huerta, everyone loves your crude analogy for helping bullies. Classic! Marlon Morgan, your wellness program is an awesome example of making a difference, and your insight was extremely helpful. Youth for Christ, I love what you do for schools, and your Point Break program is truly making an impact. All schools should offer it. Doug, Kim, Amy, and the countless other principals and teachers I interviewed, thanks for your amazing ideas of what works. . .and your honesty about what doesn't.

I can't even being to name all of "the bullied" I interviewed. Thanks so much to all of you; you know who you are! I share your tears! Wes, and Kayla. . .you especially. Thanks for your brutal honesty.

And I am equally grateful to my team of readers who screened this book for me before it went to print, offering bold criticism and helping me chisel and refine it to what it is. You all offered so much great insight. I'm truly blessed to have such a team.

And thanks to the Kill Jon Club—you know who you are—for making me who I am. I'm better because of it. Are you?

INTRODUCTION
BULLIED, BULLY, BYSTANDER

It's 6:37 a.m., and I haven't slept for hours.

This has been an emotional project for me, probably the toughest I've ever tackled. Not because the research has been any more burdensome or the topic more daunting, but because never have I heard so much anguish and hurt.

This morning I'm sorting through hundreds of surveys and stories from the personal interviews I've conducted over the last few months—a bizarre collection of voices:

Therapists and counselors working with hurting young people.

Moms and dads who desperately want to help but are learning through trial and error.

Youth workers who are hanging out with teens on the front lines.

Teens and tweens who feel like no one understands.

Jocks.

Nerds.

Mean girls.

Band kids.

Special needs kids.

Rich, poor, overweight, anemic, gorgeous, awkward. . .the whole gamut.

All these assorted people have two common denominators: a mobile device they admittedly spend too much time on, and a story about the hurt they've seen or experienced when someone is repeatedly cruel to another. (You'll be hearing much more from me on each of those two factors.)

Welcome to the world of twenty-first-century bullying!

As the stories poured in, I began hearing familiar testimonies, almost as if there is a secret manual somewhere on how to belittle others:

- "He knocked my binder out of my hands every chance he had."

- "They told me I might as well go kill myself."
- "She posted pictures of me with the caption, 'Whore!'"

There are carbon-copy experiences on almost every campus across America.

THE BULLIED

These stories are closer to home than you might think.

It's one thing researching these stories from a safe distance, reading articles and studies about young people who were tormented daily, some who committed suicide or lashed out in violence. But I found it even more haunting to sit across the table from individuals who can hardly verbalize their own story without becoming emotional as they reveal how they were targeted by their classmates.

These kids are at the school just down the street from you.

Like the boy who had several other boys chase him down and actually try to cut off his hair. A teen girl whose classmates posted exactly how "worthless" she was on social media and how "everyone" at school hated her. Or the overweight twentysomething college student who struggled to tell me about the guys in the locker room who aggressively grabbed at his "man boobs," making cruel jokes I dare not even put into print.

As one young man finished verbalizing a painful incident he'd experienced, he finally declared, "That stuff [messes] you up forever!" (I'm paraphrasing.) After another young woman shared about the people who used to torment her, she admitted, "There are people I hate, and I haven't seen them in fifteen years."

I'm amazed how young the bullying begins. A sixth-grade girl recounted stories of when she was in fourth grade and other girls began calling her fat. One of her classmates was ruthless, daily calling her "Fatty"

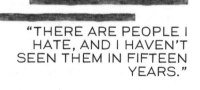

"THERE ARE PEOPLE I HATE, AND I HAVEN'T SEEN THEM IN FIFTEEN YEARS."

or asking, "Oh my gawd, how much do you weigh?" Certain insults resounded in this young girl's head, along with images she couldn't shake, like when a classmate leaned over to her and said, "When you sit down and I look at your legs, it's so disgusting."

Insults like these tend to stick in a person's psyche. I heard countless individuals recite exact words that were said over ten years ago.

And now, after hearing so many young people's agonizing stories and witnessing their pain, I can't get their voices out of my head.

Maybe it's because it brings back my own painful memories from childhood, my whole class laughing and whispering. My experiences with bullying occurred over thirty years ago, yet I still have dreams of specific faces ridiculing me publicly.

I wonder.

Do they remember my face?

Do they realize what they did to me emotionally?

Do they know I almost took my own life?

Sometimes in these dreams I lash out in rage, even violence, waking up suddenly, my heart racing.

Deep angst.

Honestly, some unresolved issues.

THE BULLY

But I think the most intriguing part of this project for me was interviewing the bullies at the helm of all this torture and pain. I found them two ways: first, asking teachers and youth workers if they knew any bullies and interviewing them anonymously. Some of these kids didn't even know they were bullies, or they never thought of it in those terms. They knew they were mean and took advantage of others, but had never put a title to it.

Second, I sought out bullies by casting a broad net on social media, asking honestly:

> *Awkward question: but were any of you bullies? Not necessarily beating up kids and stealing their lunch*

> money, *but being repeatedly cruel to someone online or face to face?*

And the responses started pouring in.

These bullies of the past all shared one thing in common. Guilt.

I guess that's where I was a little surprised. As a guy who had been on the receiving end, I was taken aback to hear so much hurt and shame from those who had been on the inflicting end.

One guy who was a jock, using his size to intimidate others smaller than him—which was practically everybody—confessed to me story after story of harassing others and belittling them publicly. "I enjoyed seeing others in pain to mask my own," he admitted.

So much regret.

His last words to me were, "Oh man, I wish I had a time machine."

Don't we all?

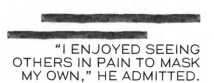

"I ENJOYED SEEING OTHERS IN PAIN TO MASK MY OWN," HE ADMITTED.

THE BYSTANDER

But then I began hearing from a third group. Not *bullies*, not the *bullied*. . .but a group I began labeling as *bystanders*. These are the kids who either laughed along or simply turned away and pretended they didn't see it. I think the majority of kids on any given school campus fall into this category today. Some have even contacted me through the years. Like my friend "Denise."

I went to school with Denise from fourth grade through high school. Denise and I were in most classes together, on a debate team together, even rode the bus to and from school together. Denise witnessed most of the ridicule I endured. When one of the few bullies in the class would knock my books off the desk or broadcast a quick insult at my expense, she did what most of the class did. She laughed along.

A few years ago I wrote an article about bullying and shared my story. The next day I received the following private message on Facebook:

With tears in my eyes, I owe you an apology. This morning I read your article, and I felt a unique twinge in my spine when I read how you still remember the jeers and pokes from your classmates back in middle school. The dam broke. I was one of those horrible kids who bullied you. While I may not have been the worst, I did it. I've thought about it a lot since coming to Christ, but when I read your post this morning. . .ouch. As I read it through tears to my hubby he said, "Sounds like you need to apologize to someone and ask for their forgiveness." He's right. Jon, I apologize for being one of those kids. and I ask for your forgiveness.—Denise

Interesting that in hindsight she perceived her laughing and joining in as "bullying."

Denise wasn't the only one experiencing regret. As I interviewed more "bystanders," I saw more tears, some from people who wanted to reach out to people from the past to beg for forgiveness but, unlike Denise, couldn't find them.

Pain seems to be the common denominator all around. Bullied, bully, bystander. . .hurt isn't partial.

> PAIN SEEMS TO BE THE COMMON DENOMINATOR ALL AROUND. BULLIED, BULLY, BYSTANDER. . .HURT ISN'T PARTIAL.

THE BREAKTHROUGH

How do we break through the pain and the emotional walls and actually help individuals from all three of these groups?

Are bullies destined to be bullies forever?

Is there hope and healing for the bullied?

Do bystanders have to just stand by. . .or can they be encouraged and equipped to stand up and do something?

What does real help look like in a world where everyone carries a device in their pocket, in their classrooms, even into their bedroom at night—a device noting exactly how many friends, likes, and follows they have at any moment. . .a connection to exactly what other people think of them and comment about them. . .a real-time barometer of their self-esteem? (Is it any wonder anxiety, depression, and suicide are all at an all-time high in the US right now?[1])

What does real help actually look like today?

Those are the questions I sought to answer. Not just as a researcher who has been studying the effects of social media and mobile devices on young people, not just as a youth worker who has witnessed mean kids regularly, and not just as a parent of a kid who was bullied so bad we had to switch schools, but also as someone who knows firsthand what it's like to endure daily ridicule and torture.

How can we break through?

CHAPTER 1
VIEW FROM THE EDGE
They don't know

Sticks and stone may break my bones,
but words will never hurt me.

We've all heard it. We all had teachers who reiterated it.

"*. . .words will never hurt me.*"

Complete foolishness.

Nothing could be further from the truth. I probably don't even need to give you thirteen reasons why.

Anyone who has been mocked or victimized will tell you nothing is more crushing or more demoralizing. Speaking completely candidly, I'd rather get beaten senseless than become the victim of public humiliation—because sadly, I've been there.

That's the intriguing thing about bullying. I've read countless articles and studies, heard theories from well-known psychologists. I've attended assemblies and conferences about bullying. . .*almost always by someone who hasn't been bullied.*

They don't know.

They really don't.

———

I grew up five minutes from the American River Parkway, a beautiful recreation area where the American River glides 120 miles from the Sierra Nevada Mountains down to the Sacramento River. One of the trails we took as kids would bring us to the edge of a cliff 120 feet high overlooking the north side of the river. Sacramento residents call it "The Bluffs." A romantic lookout for many, but for me, a location where I would contemplate taking my own life.

When I was sixteen years old I stood at the edge of that cliff staring down at the rocks below.

I can't tell you what was unique about this particular day. I honestly had experienced hundreds of days like this, especially years prior in middle school, being mocked, pushed around, and demoralized while my classmates looked on with laughter or passive approval.

I don't blame them. You had only three choices: laugh, ignore, or say something. Those who spoke up would only be next. . .so everyone chose either laughter or silence.

Literally everyone.

No one ever spoke up.

I probably couldn't have put words to what I was feeling standing on that ledge: loneli-

NO ONE EVER SPOKE UP.

ness, hurt. . .a longing for someone who understood? Most of the people in my life didn't even know what went on at my school every day. It's not their fault; I never really shared the experiences. If I did, I most likely wouldn't have even used the word *bullying*, because in my mind bullying was a big kid cornering a little kid and stealing his lunch money. My aggressors weren't big kids. They weren't even all male. My aggressors came in all shapes and sizes. But what I was experiencing was actually textbook bullying.

The Centers for Disease Control and Prevention defines *bullying* as "any unwanted aggressive behavior(s) by another youth or group of youths who are not siblings or current dating partners that involves an observed or perceived power imbalance and is repeated multiple times or is highly likely to be repeated."[1]

"Perceived power imbalance"—a good word choice. Kids don't have a positive concept of "self," so they try to make themselves feel better by hurling verbal onslaughts at others. That's an accurate description of what my peers did to me each day. I was an easy target, so I became a stepping-stone others used to raise themselves up so they could feel more powerful.

"Repeated multiple times"—also accurate. For me it was daily in middle school, at least weekly in high school. Certain environments seemed to foster it more than others, none more so than PE class.

That particular day began with gym class, physical education, or PE as our school called it. PE is a cruel requirement for nonathletes, something the physically fit will never understand. PE is where the weak get intimidated by the strong. PE is where small boys get hung by their underwear or slapped in the back of the legs while bystanders laugh hysterically.

That morning in PE a popular kid had said something cruel. I don't remember the exact exchange, but knowing me, I probably retaliated with a quick verbal jab. I had developed a quick wit over the years. I had plenty of experience defending myself.

But this kid wasn't going to tolerate any banter. He hit me hard in the jaw. I can still hear the cackles from the crowd and feel the stares of those who quickly circled around. Funny, I don't recall the physical pain of the hit.

More words were exchanged. I had two choices: fight or back down. I chose to back down.

Social suicide.

Names were called—cruel names that are difficult even to put into print.

"Pu**y!"

"Fag!"

I was neither, but it didn't matter.

Threats were made. "You'd better watch your back!"

He meant it. And he was right. This altercation had triggered a social seismic shift, and there were aftershocks. You see, once someone is publicly humiliated, the victim bears an invisible KICK ME sign on his back. For the rest of the day I endured shoves, jeers, and cruel whispers from kids I had never even met. Other kids with low self-esteem jumped on the opportunity to step up a notch on the social ladder by lowering someone else a rung.

ONCE SOMEONE IS PUBLICLY HUMILIATED, THE VICTIM BEARS AN INVISIBLE "KICK ME" SIGN ON HIS BACK.

I don't know why this particular day pushed me over the tipping point, since I had experienced many other days like it. Regardless, six hours after the original jab, I stood at the edge of the cliff looking down at the rocks.

Should I jump?

I wanted to jump. I really wanted to, honestly, for selfish reasons.

I'll show them.

They'll regret everything they ever said!

BROKEN

Something happens to kids when they are repeatedly mocked and pushed around publicly. It changes them. It happened to my dad, and it happened to me. But the hardest by far was to see it happen to my son, Alec.

When Alec was in fifth grade, we noticed a dramatic change in him over a period of just four weeks.

Our family had just moved across town, and we enrolled our three kids in a new school. The girls adjusted fine, but Alec immediately became a target of harassment. It happened daily. We saw it on his face the first day we picked him up. We asked him what happened.

"Some kids teased me," he said.

We did what most parents do. We told him not to worry about what other kids say.

See—I did it too. "Ignore it." It's a common parental response (so common I'm focusing my entire next chapter on it).

We were dead wrong.

My wife, Lori, and I watched a sweet, innocent, gregarious boy gradually chiseled down to a repressed, dejected little kid. Bitterness began to emerge. His posture literally changed. Previously he walked with confidence and a little bounce to his step. Just a few weeks later, his shoulders drooped and his head hung low, almost as if he was scared to look around.

It's sad to see what bullying does to a kid. My dad and I both eventually recognized it in Alec. He was emotionally broken. We knew it all too well—we both had been there.

My dad is five foot four as an adult. So as you can imagine, as a kid he was small—plus he was shy and a little on the pudgy side. It doesn't take too many times hearing the words "fat" or "midget" thrown at you to develop a complex about your weight and size.

Kids don't even need physical imperfections to be bullied, but if you have a major physical flaw, you're a prime target. My buck teeth provided plenty of ammo for everyone. I shudder even typing those words—*buck teeth*. It seemed as though not a day went by that I didn't hear them.

My baby teeth were fine. But when my permanent teeth came in. . .wow! It's literally too much to describe; just flip the book over and take a peek at the picture on the back cover. Yeah, that's me in fourth grade.

I heard it every day.

"Hey, Bugs Bunny!"

"Buck-toothed beaver!"

"Chicklets!"

"Hey, can opener!" (You gotta give creativity points to whoever came up with this insult.)

And I didn't just hear it from mockers—I heard it from little kids in the grocery store!

"Mommy, what's wrong with that kid's teeth?"

"Don't stare, honey."

You wouldn't believe the things I heard.

When people poked fun at me, I always hoped adults would intervene. But my confidence in adults quickly faded.

Most adults didn't notice the jesting and teasing. Some actually laughed. In fourth grade I was at a basketball camp when a group of kids cornered me, making fun of my teeth. I remember trying to retort; I don't recall what I had planned on saying, because I never finished my sentence. All I could manage was something like, "Oh yeah, well I can do something you can't. . ."

MOST ADULTS DIDN'T NOTICE THE JESTING AND TEASING. SOME ACTUALLY LAUGHED.

And my coach quickly interjected, "Yeah! Chew through wood!"

Once an adult opens that door, it never shuts. No one at that camp called me by name again. I was "Beaver" or "Woody Woodchuck." (Isn't it nice when nicknames are memorable little tongue twisters that kids can all shout together?)

Those who haven't been mocked or teased might not understand the repercussions of nicknames like this. No, for me these labels were not just cute nicknames. They were a badge. Each name was a sign saying OPEN SEASON, and I was an eight-point buck. For the rest of that week I was mocked, shoved, and threatened. Everyone knew it was socially acceptable to demoralize Woody Woodchuck.

"Hey, Woody, why don't you chuck this wood!"

So when my son was being bullied, I knew what he was experiencing.

When I talked with the principal, I provided her with specifics. After all, it wasn't just boys who were picking on Alec. A girl in his class had just turned around in her chair the day prior, leaned on his desk, and said, "Wow, you are the ugliest kid I've ever seen. Your mom must wonder, *Why is my kid so ugly?*"

I shared this incident with the principal. She didn't seem to process it. I wish I would have had a hidden video camera in her office. She didn't address any of the specifics I shared; instead she bragged, "Our school doesn't tolerate any bullying."

She actually showed me a banner hanging in the cafeteria: OUR SCHOOL IS BULLY-FREE, THE WAY IT'S MEANT TO BE.

These Bully-Free signs and banners are becoming even more common in schools across the country today. Google it. You can buy them all over the web, "to send a positive message and inspire students to think before they act."

Really?

I'd love to see that data and hear those testimonies: "There I was, about to knock the books out of Eugene's hands. . .but then I looked up and saw a poster. . ."

My son, Alec, and I still talk about that useless banner to this day.

Alec got to the point where some kids started pushing him and slapping the back of his neck. It was so hard for Lori and me to hear the terrible accounts day after day. Finally I told Alec, "You don't have to take that. You can stand up for yourself."

Alec looked up at me with his big blue eyes, his lip quivering, and said, "I don't want to get into trouble."

I told him, "You won't get in trouble from me!"

Maybe that was just another victim talking. I don't even know if it was good advice. Lori questioned my reasoning. "Are you sure that's what he should do? Or is that just someone who was bullied as a kid talking?"

It was a fair question.

Fight or flight. Those are the two natural responses to confrontation. We decided to encourage him to seek "flight." In fact, we switched schools. He got plugged in with a group of really creative kids—like him—at his new school and at church. But we also enrolled him in martial arts to try to boost his confidence.

Some of Alec's scars slowly began to heal. That is. . .until the first week of middle school when some kids started pushing him around.

I'll give you one guess as to where this happened. . .

During PE.

During PE as Alec ran around the track, two boys would stop him and tell him, "You can't pass." Of course, the teacher was nowhere to be found.

Note to teachers and administrators: It's hard to be "bully-free, the way it's meant to be" like your banner says when gym class is a free-for-all for big kids. (Don't even get me started on "picking teams." I still have dreams about standing there alone, the last one chosen.)

I didn't want to lose all the ground we had gained with Alec, so I asked him more about the situation. "Can you avoid these kids? Can you run somewhere else?"

Flight.

It's always good to avoid the situation as best as possible. But the confrontation with these two bullies was unavoidable. Day after day they found Alec when the teacher wasn't around—which was a lot!

I looked Alec in the eye and told him, "Alec, if those kids push you or corner you, hit them in the nose as hard as you can, and don't stop swinging until someone pulls you off!"

Fight.

Let me add a quick disclaimer here. I'm not advising you to defer to violence. In today's day of lawsuits, you'll probably get sued.

But I honestly didn't care.

They had poked Mama Bear. . .er. . .Papa Bear one too many times, and frankly I was ready to go down to the school and start tossing kids around. I was one straw short of grabbing the keys and telling Lori, "Call our lawyer—I'm going to be arrested in about thirty minutes!"

But my advice to Alec that day was to swing away.

Alec was shocked. "I thought I wasn't supposed to fight."

"Defending yourself is way different than fighting, Alec," I assured him. "If they bully you, you go *Christmas Story* on them!"

"But Dad, I'll get suspended."

I leaned in close to my boy. "If you get suspended for defending yourself, Alec, I'll take the day off work and take you out for ice cream, and then we'll hang out and have fun all day. You won't get in trouble from me for defending yourself. You'll get rewarded."

I didn't know if I was giving Alec sound advice, but speaking candidly as a father, I'll confess that desperate situations sometimes generate desperate responses. At the time, I just wanted Alec to know that we were in his corner no matter what. And I hoped to provide him with the freedom to defend himself.

The next day when Lori brought Alec home from school, he looked apprehensive.

"What happened?" I asked.

Alec was looking down at the ground while he talked. "I got sent to the principal's office for fighting."

This might sound strange, but *I was so proud of him*! I smiled and gave him a big hug. "Sweet! Let's go for ice cream!"

Over ice cream, Alec told me the whole story. The kids stopped him on the track again and didn't let him pass. Alec tried to go around, but one of the kids pushed him. Alec swallowed hard and started swinging. He knew how to hit. He hit one guy to the ground and the other grabbed him. Alec somehow managed to get the other kid in a headlock and started punching him as well. The punching turned to rolling on the ground. Next thing he knew, all three of them found themselves in the principal's office.

The principal knew the other two kids by name; he didn't know Alec. Alec told him his story. The principal said, "I don't want to see you in here again. You can go." Then he kept the other two in his office.

Apparently a couple of Alec's hits landed pretty hard, because the next day one of those two kids came to school with a black eye.

Alec didn't have any more physical confrontations that year.

I wish I could tell you that Alec's remaining years were bully-free. They weren't. He joined wrestling the next year in middle school, and that really helped. But during his freshman year of high school, bullies actually sat in the hallway and threw pieces of muffins at certain kids, calling them names. Alec said it happened all the time, not just to him, but to numerous kids. He just tried his best to avoid those hallways.

So was it over?

The question Lori and I had was, would all these experiences have long-term effects? Or is the idiom true: ". . .but words will never hurt me"?

I had definitely experienced long-term effects, and apparently I'm not alone. Every time I interviewed an adult who had experienced severe bullying, I heard the same things.

- "I'm still tentative in social situations."
- "Whenever people are talking with each other at work, I can't help but wonder if they're talking about me."
- "I am still dealing with what those experiences have done to me. Depression, suicidal thoughts. . ."

Words will never hurt me?

REPERCUSSIONS

I've seen it hundreds of times in over two decades of youth ministry. Bullied kids are more socially tentative, sometimes skeptical of social situations, fearful of rejection. I've seen many of them become prejudiced toward certain social circles: jocks or popular kids.

This social trepidation often causes bullied kids to push others away. Even if other kids are nice or give them a chance, the bullied don't like to let others "in." They've been burned before.

I can relate. I did the same thing, even into my college years. My skepticism toward people sometimes resulted in bitterness and quarrelling. If you met anyone who attended college with me my freshman year, they'd probably describe me as tense, insecure, and easily aggravated.

The stereotypical bullied kid is often guarded, defensive, and, as a result, socially awkward.

Today the situation is only worsened by technology. Not just because kids are mocked on social media, but because technology offers socially awkward kids a place to escape social situations, which only cripples their social skills. Technology also provides a false sense of "friendship" with people who aren't always positive influences. It becomes a downward spiral.

The pattern looks like this:

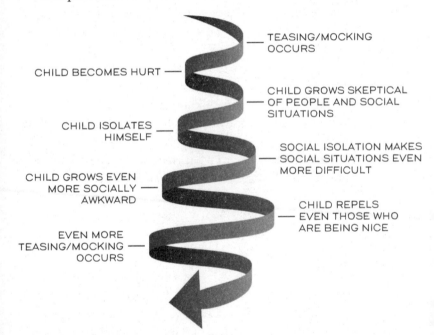

TEASING/MOCKING OCCURS

CHILD BECOMES HURT

CHILD GROWS SKEPTICAL OF PEOPLE AND SOCIAL SITUATIONS

CHILD ISOLATES HIMSELF

SOCIAL ISOLATION MAKES SOCIAL SITUATIONS EVEN MORE DIFFICULT

CHILD GROWS EVEN MORE SOCIALLY AWKWARD

CHILD REPELS EVEN THOSE WHO ARE BEING NICE

EVEN MORE TEASING/MOCKING OCCURS

That's why the fix isn't easy. Preventing bullying requires more than a school assembly. I appreciate some of today's antibullying initiatives, but it takes more than a nice kid inviting a less popular kid to sit with him at lunch once.

Healing takes time. But it's hard to heal when the scab keeps getting ripped off day after day.

Bullying happens more often than you might think. Most adults just don't realize bullying's pervasive reach. One study found that 50 percent of US high schoolers said they had "bullied, teased, or taunted someone at least once."[2] Let that sink in for a moment. Half of the kids at the campus down the street from you admit to belittling others.

I believe it. Today's young people have poor self-esteem and little to no conflict-management skills, a double-edged sword that easily cuts down others. When a bully feels low about himself, he cuts others down lower. If someone else bothers him in any way, he responds negatively. Why? He has self-esteem issues and doesn't know how to respond. The same study revealed that 37 percent of boys agreed that it was okay to "hit or threaten" a person who angered them.

I APPRECIATE SOME OF TODAY'S ANTIBULLYING INITIATIVES, BUT IT TAKES MORE THAN A NICE KID INVITING A LESS POPULAR KID TO SIT WITH HIM AT LUNCH ONCE.

Who is teaching this kind of conflict resolution? This isn't self-defense, mind you; this is just, "If someone frustrates you, hit 'em!"

This destructive cycle results in certain kids, usually the ones at the bottom of the pecking order, getting emotionally hurt.

So how do the bullied typically respond?

The most common response from bullied kids I've observed is withdrawal. Those of us who have been bullied will assure you that *the safest place is alone.*

ISOLATION

Bullying victims seek refuge in a variety of arenas. I always retreated to home, where I could be creative by writing and drawing. I played piano as a child (yeah, I was the entire "nerd" package), so during some of the rough years I began to write songs. In retrospect, I don't think they were very good, but they were therapeutic. And anyone reading the lyrics even today would gain insight into bullying victims' emotions.

My daughters recently looked through one of my "memory boxes" stuffed in the closet under the stairway. After paging through my yearbooks and drawings, they came across a folder with a bunch of my music. They saw some of the lyrics I wrote and asked me candidly, "Dad, were you serious?"

Here are the lyrics they found:

> *Alone I am waiting*
> *Nobody caring*
> *This life isn't for me. . .*
>
> *Is anyone out there*
> *Someone who cares?*
> *Someone whose feelings and thoughts I can share?*
> *There has to be someone*
> *Someone who feels like me*

A bridge was scratched out near the bottom:

> *This life isn't wanted*
> *I might as well end it*

I don't recall having suicidal thoughts frequently, but I remember feeling completely alone at times and wondering if anyone understood. I longed to meet others—even one person—who felt like me. But I didn't know where to find this person.

Looking back, I'm thankful I didn't have social media to retreat to in search of "friends" who understood. With my obsessive personality, I probably never would have been more than five feet from my mobile device.

Turns out I wasn't alone in my feelings. Even today, all over the world, ostracized teenagers are looking for camaraderie wherever and however they can find it. Sadly, these lonely kids don't always find what they're looking for, so they resort to self-medication. A recent report out of the journal *Pediatrics* revealed that kids who are bullied in early adolescence may be more likely to use drugs or alcohol in their teens. Valerie A. Earnshaw, PhD, of Boston Children's Hospital, and colleagues wrote, "Indeed, a small but growing body of work suggests that early experiences of peer victimization are linked to worse mental health and greater engagement in health risk behaviors during early adulthood."[3]

This report is only one of many showing the lasting ramifications of bullying. A study of kids in the United States, Canada, and France found that victims of bullying are more likely to report depression, low self-esteem, poor school performance, and suicide attempts. These kids, described as "by far the most socially ostracized by their peers," were "most likely to display conduct problems, least engaged in school, and they also reported elevated levels of depression and loneliness."[4]

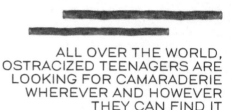

ALL OVER THE WORLD, OSTRACIZED TEENAGERS ARE LOOKING FOR CAMARADERIE WHEREVER AND HOWEVER THEY CAN FIND IT

I shuddered when I first read that study because it described me perfectly. *Conduct problems, least engaged in school, lonely.*

I remember talking with a few adults, revealing just a little of what I was experiencing. I wasn't about to tell them what I really felt.

The fact is, words do hurt. In fact, they played over and over again in my head on repeat, like a skipping CD.

Maybe we need to rethink the whole "sticks and stones" idiom.

But "sticks and stones" isn't the only little phrase I've heard minimizing this kind of hurt. In fact, I'm going to devote the entire next chapter to the one I've heard the most.

DISCUSSION QUESTIONS

1. Why did you pick up this book?

2. What was one thing in this chapter that really stood out to you?

3. Jonathan suggested that young people have three choices when they see someone being bullied: laugh, ignore it, or say something. Which did you typically choose?

4. In the definition of bullying by the Centers for Disease Control, bullying is limited to youth "who are not siblings or current dating partners." Why do you think this is? What is bully-like behavior called in those settings?

5. Jonathan confessed that he advised his son, "Alec, if those kids push you or corner you, hit them in the nose as hard as you can, and don't stop swinging until someone pulls you off!" What do you think of this advice?

6. Jonathan described the downward spiral that begins when a child gets teased, becomes hurt, grows skeptical of people and social situations, and gradually isolates himself, which makes social situations more difficult, which makes the child even more socially awkward, which repels people more, and then more teasing occurs. Have you observed this spiral? What did you notice?

7. How can you tell the difference between shy kids and kids who are slowly beginning to isolate themselves in an unhealthy way?

8. How can you do a better job of noticing the signs of bullying this week?

CHAPTER 2
JUST IGNORE IT
Trees falling in the forest

If a tree falls in a forest and no one is there
to hear it, does it make a sound?

"Ignore them and they'll ignore you."

This is obviously the advice of someone who has never experienced daily torment from their peers.

It's nearly impossible to ignore the entire class when they're all laughing at you.

I was thirteen years old when I first considered taking my own life. I never told my parents or my teachers about these feelings. I never shared the extent of what kids were saying and doing to me because it was embarrassing. In fact, it was actually a little unbelievable.

IT'S NEARLY IMPOSSIBLE TO IGNORE THE ENTIRE CLASS WHEN THEY'RE ALL LAUGHING AT YOU.

In eighth grade, a kid I'll call "Dennis" actually started the Kill Jon Club. Absurd as it sounds, they actually made T-shirts with a gun sight drawn over a caricature of my face and the initials KJC. Four kids wore the shirts to school. The rest of the class laughed hysterically.

The teachers didn't have a clue.

Let that sink in for a moment. *The teachers didn't have a clue.*

How can a teacher miss an entire class laughing at one kid, knocking his books off his desk, smacking his neck when they walk by, and actually wearing T-shirts with a picture of a gun scope on his face?

I finally did tell an adult about everything that happened. I'll never forget her response when I told her, "They made T-shirts":

"No, they didn't."

She actually told me it *didn't* happen. She thought I was making it up.

Was this some freak occurrence?

Let's fast-forward thirty years to the present.

NO ONE DID ANYTHING

An overweight boy called "lard-a**" daily.

A girl who was physically assaulted because she liked the wrong guy.

A crowd of kids taunting a kid with a prominent red birthmark on his face: "Hey, Kool-Aid!"

An overweight girl named Carla heartlessly labeled Cowla, simply trying to navigate around campus without being mooed at day after day.

These are just a few of the voices I heard as I began interviewing young people about the way they were treated at school. Hundreds of young people surveyed. . .and the one common denominator I kept hearing over and over again:

"No one did anything."

I don't want to be an alarmist, and I definitely don't want to insinuate that parents, teachers, and principals don't care. I've interviewed countless caring adults. I've met with counselors who recognize the problem and are striving to come alongside hurting kids. I've attended assemblies, even all-day programs proactively addressing the issue and providing caring adults to follow up.

But somehow kids are being missed. Many—dare I say *most*—of these kids' voices are being drowned out in the crowd. Too many adults simply don't have a clue what's going on.

Literally every story I've heard contains the same element:

- "I told the adult on yard duty, and they said to just ignore it."
- "I told my parents, and they dismissed it."
- "I told the principal, and he called the boys in and warned them. Nothing changed."

I don't have any problem believing these stories, because I've experienced all of this firsthand.

So let me ask this: in a world full of caring adults, how is it that we keep missing the cries of hurting kids?

The communication channels in many of today's school systems need a total revamp. A youth worker I know told me a story of her daughter being bullied in eighth grade so severely that she ended up seeing a counselor and suffering depression.

No one likes me. I'm not good enough.

The mom didn't find out until the end of the year when an incident occurred where parents were finally contacted.

"This is the first I've heard of it," she told the principal.

The principal just backpedaled.

The same mom ran into some teachers at the school over the summer, and they offered their condolences. "Wow, the situation was really bad. I don't know how she made it through the year."

No one had reported a thing the entire year.

Why is it that a teacher would assume someone else was handling it?

Why is it so many of us just become "bystanders" who don't want to get involved?

How can we miss crowds of kids at recess hurling insults at an autistic kid? How is it that in a high school locker room kids are constantly ridiculed, tormented, slapped on the back of the legs, even hung up by their underwear? How can an entire campus know that there is going to be a fight after school—*and adults actually be warned about it*—and yet a kid gets chased by a mob and beaten to the ground until needing to be hospitalized, while campus security tosses a football back and forth? These are all very true stories.

As I embarked on this research, I was pretty confident I had a grasp on the issue, having worked with teenagers for the last twenty-five years. But honestly, I was surprised how I kept hearing the same story over and over again. . .the story of a young person crying out for help and an adult saying, "Just ignore it." It was the one phrase that seemed to appear in almost every interview. A kid cried out for help, and his or her voice was dismissed by an adult.

The adult responses came in many different forms. Let me share one specific example involving Lindsey, the daughter of a friend of mine. The story began like many: Lindsey liked a boy, but another girl also liked the boy, so this girl began humiliating Lindsey out of jealousy and spite. She and her friends ganged up on Lindsey, making subtle comments as they passed her in the hallways, reaching through the crowd and knocking her books out of her hands, even pulling her hair. At junior prom, Lindsey wore a dress that tied in the back. In the crowd a hand reached out and untied the back of her dress, causing it to fall down in the front.

One day Lindsey was knocked to the ground and threatened, so much so that she feared for her safety. She fled to the bathroom, hid in a stall, and texted her mom: "Mom, please come get me. I'm scared."

Her mom rushed to school and told the front office what happened. "My daughter was just threatened by a group of girls and is now hiding in the bathroom terrified. She just texted me from a stall."

Wanna guess what the lady at the front office responded?

"She's not supposed to be texting at school."

As I share stories like this with my friends in the school systems, they are horrified. "That would *never* happen at our school."

Are you sure?

Are you absolutely positive that the person supervising the playground is truly keeping watch, or is there a chance they're just hanging out with a select tribe of kids? Are you sure you're aware of what's truly going on with your kids at school or in the most popular place today's mean kids ridicule others: social media?

I missed many of the signs with my son, and I had experienced bullying myself at his age.

Why are we missing these cues?

As I reflect on those painful years when kids humiliated me every day, I realize I never said a word. I just became more removed and isolated. No one would eat lunch with me. After all, it would have been social suicide.

The one saving grace was at 2:43 p.m. the bell rang and I got to go home where I was loved and encouraged. It was safe. . .*for about fifteen hours.* Then I had to go back to school and live it all over again.

Today when the bell rings, kids might leave their school campus, but they can never escape the other world, a world where mockers and intimidators thrive. Ironically, they carry a gateway to that world right in their pockets with them, because they see that world as an avenue of escape—but in reality it's putting them in bondage.

Kids across the globe are searching for friendship with someone who understands them. Often their search leads them to social media, the gaming world, anywhere they can connect with someone. . .from a distance.

THEY CARRY A GATEWAY TO THAT WORLD RIGHT IN THEIR POCKETS WITH THEM.

But it's not working. Social media isn't filling the void. In fact, it's making things worse (more on this to come). The voices of the bullied are still unheard.

Even at church.

NOWHERE SAFE

I wish I could tell you that youth groups are always a safe place. I'm a huge believer in young people finding connection, and church is one of the greatest places to do that. But let's not rush to assume that everyone at church is as loving as Jesus.

Our church was always a great place of love and acceptance for me as a young teenager, so I assumed it would be for our son, Alec. Unfortunately, it didn't start that way.

In middle school Alec actually got bullied at youth group. The junior high pastor was an outstanding athlete—an amazing basketball player. As sharp as he was, he didn't have any idea what being bullied looked like. That's something I have slowly begun to observe. Many don't know what to look for.

One time Alec went to a church winter camp—three days in the snow with middle school kids and a few counselors. This camp had about a one-to-seven ratio of adults to kids.

Sounds pretty safe, right?

Alec was teased and ostracized by the other guys in his cabin every time the counselors weren't around. His solution was to withdraw by himself.

Alec had brought a stuffed monkey to this particular weekend trip and placed it on his pillow and sleeping bag during the day. The other kids teased him about it relentlessly.

One night Alec came back to the cabin to find the monkey outside, torn and lying in the mud. Alec threw his furry little companion away, too embarrassed to tell anyone. I didn't find out about the incident until years later.

This kind of teasing happened for years, to the point that Alec didn't want to go to church. I remember feeling torn.

Am I doing the right thing making him go to youth group?

I know connection is good. . .but not this kind of connection, right?

By God's grace we moved and started attending a new church where the kids were much more loving. I hate to admit it, but the grass actually was a little greener at this new church. Alec went on a mission trip with the youth group and came back excited about all the new friends he met.

He told us about a group of guys he was hanging with. "We're bros!" he told us. Something new for him.

The church became a place of healing for him. In fact, two of his closest friends from church youth group were football players. This stretched Alec to realize that not all jocks are bullies.

Alec had to learn to saturate himself in God's grace and forgiveness so he could pass them on to others. As a result of his experiences, Alec is more empathetic to people who are picked on. He can spot them more easily than most. I've found that many who were bullied have a radar for detecting evidence of it in others. They see from an entirely different perspective.

PERSPECTIVE

I'm the same way, in both healthy and unhealthy ways. The unhealthy facet is that I'm damaged goods. .I'm much more sensitive than the average bear. And yet this sensitivity gives me a perspective that has helped me spot "loners" and victims over the years.

I remember a few years back when I was running an on-campus ministry for junior high kids. About two hundred kids were in the school gymnasium playing dodgeball when I noticed some bantering across the room. One of my volunteers and I both arrived on the scene to witness a final exchange of words between two kids: a chunky kid named Brian and a skinny kid I didn't know. When the two of them saw us, the skinny kid's expression hardly changed. He looked scared and ashamed. Brian, however, quickly metamorphosed from angry to playful. He was the first to speak up.

"Dodgeball rocks. I love it when we play dodgeball."

A blatant smokescreen.

Brian actually put his arm around the skinny kid, whose body language was screaming, "Please get me out of here!"

My volunteer, an athlete, quickly interjected, "All right. Let's get back to the game."

Brian immediately kissed up to my volunteer, and the two of them went off together. The crowd dispersed, and the skinny kid withdrew to a corner of the room. I approached him.

"You okay?" I asked.

"Yeah. Fine," he answered, never looking up.

"You like dodgeball?" Probably a stupid question.

He looked to the left and right, almost as if he was scouting out the nearest exit. "No. Not really."

At the end of the night I told my volunteers to keep an eye on those two as they exited the gym, since I would be stuck on gym duty inside.

"Why?" they asked.

"Because I think something's going down."

"Really?" my athletic volunteer asked. "Brian's cool."

Twenty minutes later while parents were picking up kids, Brian and two friends jumped the skinny kid right in front of the line of cars. . .while my volunteers were standing there talking with each other, oblivious.

Apparently during dodgeball the skinny kid had hit Brian with an embarrassingly good shot. Brian didn't like being embarrassed by a "weakling," so he felt the need to restore the power hierarchy.

I saw this on the weaker kid's face.

My volunteers didn't.

The signs were there. We failed that kid.

That's the interesting thing about bullying. Spotting it is easier when you know the perspective. Some people honestly have no idea what it feels like to be ridiculed every day. High school might have been a blast for them. Those people don't necessarily recognize bullying, and they don't think bullying is a problem.

It's like the moment on the TV show *Big Bang Theory* when the nerdy Leonard was describing a bad experience at work to his gorgeous wife, Penny.

> **Leonard:** No one would talk to me in the halls; they just glared at me. It was just like high school all over again.
> **Penny:** Oh, I would totally do high school all over again.[1]

Perhaps we need to open our eyes to the possibility that some people have had a different experience than us.

It's a skill. Stepping into someone else's shoes. Empathizing, not minimizing.

Whenever there is a school shooting, I always find it interesting to read the random quotes from kids at the school. Some classmates will say, "He wasn't bullied." Then in another interview a different kid will say, "He was bullied all the time!"

IT'S A SKILL. STEPPING INTO SOMEONE ELSE'S SHOES. EMPATHIZING, NOT MINIMIZING.

Shortly after the 2018 Parkland shooting in Florida, in which seventeen individuals were killed, the *Miami Herald* interviewed a student, asking about the shooter. The student, a classmate of the shooter, said, "Someone could have approached a faculty member, a guidance counselor, a teacher and said, 'This kid gets bullied a lot, someone should do something.' I regret definitely not saying anything."[2]

Yet others said, "I never saw him being bullied."

People tend to be quick to minimize the evidence of bullying: *I didn't see it, so it couldn't have happened.*

Even parents minimize it: "Oh, they don't hate you." "It's not that bad." "Just ignore them and they'll ignore you."

Not even close to true. And when we minimize the situation like that, we are basically telling them, "I don't care."

Do you?

Do you hear their cries for help?

Maybe we're listening in the wrong place. . . .

DISCUSSION QUESTIONS

1. What was one thing in this chapter that really stood out to you?

2. Why do you think so many bullying victims feel ignored or dismissed? Do you think they really are ignored and dismissed?

3. What do you think teachers and school administrators should do if they hear talk of a fight happening after school?

4. How do you think the front office should respond if a frantic mom shows up to school and says, "My daughter was just threatened by a group of girls and is now hiding in the bathroom terrified. She just texted me from a stall"?

5. What effects do you notice now that kids carry devices with them that are not only an avenue of escape but a gateway to bullying?

6. If bullying victims are more likely to use drugs or alcohol, experience depression, have low self-esteem, perform poorly at school, and attempt suicide, then why do adults sometimes minimize the problem by saying, "It's not that bad," or "Just ignore them"?

7. How can parents, teachers, and youth workers do a better job of spotting "loners"?

8. How should adults respond if they notice a child being teased or targeted aggressively and repeatedly?

CHAPTER 3
DIGITAL HURT
The ubiquity of cyberbullying

Haley is a school counselor at a high school in California.

She is just twenty-four years old, and she loves her phone.

I asked Haley how many of her counseling sessions have to do with phones or social media and she laughed. "Seriously?"

When she finally realized I wasn't kidding, she said, "All of them. If they aren't the cause of the conflict, then they certainly are an element in it. It's just the way young people communicate today."

"How different is it from when you were in high school just a few years ago?" I asked.

"It's a whole new world," she said. "A few years ago my friends and I enjoyed our phones—these kids can't live without them. Some of them can't sit through five minutes of my sessions without whipping out their phones like I'm not even in the room."

"How much do devices contribute to bullying?" I asked, cutting to the chase.

"They've made it far worse," Haley said. "It doesn't stop at school. It blows up overnight, and we have to defuse everything that was said for the sixteen hours they were throwing hate off campus."

"Give me an example," I said.

"Last month someone posted a 'nude' on the school's Instagram account—which they still don't know how that happened, by the way. Anyway, the picture was a selfie from the neck down and the caption said it was a sophomore girl from the school. . .which it wasn't. But that didn't matter because the whole school thought it was. She finally switched schools."

THE NEW NORMAL

Cyberbullying is a new level of hurt.

CYBERBULLYING IS A NEW LEVEL OF HURT.

Cyberbullying victims are the most likely to commit suicide. Young people who are bullied are twice as likely to contemplate suicide as their peers, but cyberbullying victims are three times as likely.[1]

What is it about cyberbullying that is pushing so many young people past the tipping point?

Digital communication experts from Common Sense Media define *cyberbullying* as "the use of digital-communication tools. . .to make another person feel angry, sad, or scared, usually again and again."[2]

The definition makes sense. It's fairly clear.

Then how come most young people don't necessarily label this kind of cruel digital communication as "cyberbullying"?

I asked a local psychologist this question, and he answered without a second thought.

"It's because they don't know anything different."

This particular therapist I interviewed works with a wellness program providing "Tier 3" counseling in local schools. That's when a student's depression or acting out becomes severe enough that the school feels the student needs to meet with a therapist. This program provides counselors who meet with the student one-on-one on campus for ten sessions, then the family for three sessions. He and his counselors deal with the repercussions of cyberbullying constantly.

"We see this all the time," he said. "Adults know what it's like to live life without tech, but students have never experienced a world without it. So the pressure of measuring up and being 'liked' is just normal for them. Yes, it's adding to their stress in unprecedented ways, but they just don't know any different."

TWO SEISMIC SHIFTS

It's easy for us to forget how different our perspective is. Most parents today were lucky to only have to endure this kind of drama or teasing from about 7:30 a.m. to 2:30 p.m. on school days. But now our kids are never free from the constant pressure of garnering "likes," enduring snarky comments, and navigating mean posts and rants. Bullies now have a platform where they can make lives miserable 24-7.

When did this begin?

Two seismic shifts in this new millennium have opened up the floodgates for bullying 24-7: the rise of social media and smartphone adoption.

THE RISE OF SOCIAL MEDIA

Social media didn't really gain traction with young people until MySpace exploded in early 2005. MySpace provided something that no other website, chatroom, or online community had perfected yet—an online community where young people could meet others, chat, and be whoever they wanted to be. In hindsight, it's strange that it took a couple of decades for anyone to figure this out.

Even though home computers began to find their way into American homes in the 1980s, chatting of any kind didn't really begin until the '90s, and even then, it was most often on a large desktop computer plugged into a phone line (some of us might remember the distinctive squawking of our 56K modem as it connected).

I worked with middle school and high school students in the early '90s, and I remember a small percentage of kids discovering online chatrooms. Most kids were aware of these online venues, but they had yet to become a huge part of youth culture. Frankly, kids were more excited about what color their new pager was.

Pagers are an interesting sidebar. Even back then young people showed a fascination with being able to "message" each other. Almost every kid I worked with (a few hundred teens a week) had a pager and would constantly get pages from friends with little codes like *411 if their friend just needed information or *911 if it was urgent. The biggest question I got from teens back then was, "Can I use your phone real quick? I got paged."

Young people loved mobile communication. But online communication and mobile communication had yet to meet.

Back in the online world, the first social media site was Six Degrees, created in 1997.[3] This site allowed users to create a profile and make friends. This site was followed by some blogging sites, but social media didn't get going until MySpace and LinkedIn gained momentum in the early 2000s.

Overnight MySpace became an unmonitored playground where kids flocked to post whatever they wanted to whoever they wanted. . .and parents didn't have a clue. The site quickly became a favorite for pedophiles, like the high school teacher accused of making sexual advances to a fourteen-year-old girl on the internet, later arrested on computer pornography charges. The *Tampa Bay Times* contends that William Warren Greico, forty-two, "first approached the girl after he saw her posting on myspace.com."[4]

Sadly, this wasn't a unique event. *Saturday Night Live* even aired a sketch mocking this danger, with Andy Samberg teaching a "MySpace and You" night class at a community college where one mom and about a dozen pedophiles attended, all asking questions like, "So no one monitors this website? Excellent!"

I remember giving MySpace seminars to parents at this time, helping them understand the dangers of this new platform where literally anyone could be anyone in this fascinating new cyberworld where people scrolled through pictures looking for someone to chat with.

But still teens couldn't get enough of this fun new way to "cruise" a strip populated with 99 percent young people.

MySpace drew teens to computers like locusts. I couldn't even print out my airline's boarding passes at hotels anymore because unattended teens and tweens would be hovering around the one or two online terminals provided by the hotel for "businesspeople." Library computers weren't used for research anymore; they were yet another location where kids could browse MySpace. Anywhere a kid could find a computer with a connection. Social media hadn't gone mobile yet.

In 2005 MySpace was the seventh most popular English-speaking site on the web, beat out only by Yahoo, Google, Amazon, and a few others.[5] But users didn't notice that #38 on the list of sites was another social media site rapidly gaining popularity. It required a college email address. The site was called Facebook.

Facebook launched on February 4, 2004, but only for select people at Harvard. The online community eventually expanded to other colleges in the greater Boston area, and soon the whole nation wanted in. By 2006 the site was available to everyone age thirteen and older with a valid email address. By 2008 there were 100 million users. . .and MySpace was abandoned as quickly as it had emerged.[6]

MySpace who?

Meanwhile, the world was about to experience the second seismic shift that would open the door to 24-7 online access: the rise of the smartphone.

SMARTPHONE ADOPTION

As much as young people craved online communities like MySpace and Facebook, these online venues had yet to go mobile. In 2005 mobile communication and social media were two completely separate entities. Kids were either online on a computer connected to a wall or texting their friends on a phone. Pagers were so yesterday at this point, and texting was everything they could ever want (so they thought).

The biggest conversation among parents at this time was their kids' obsession with texting. At first mobile providers charged per text, and that caused huge problems with families. Mom would open the AT&T bill and discover over four hundred dollars in texting charges. News outlets featured stories about kids texting three thousand–plus text messages per month. The amount of texts a kid texted almost became bragging rights. Mobile services quickly began offering "free text messaging."

Meanwhile, technology was gaining speed in every area. New phones with new features were emerging each month. New entertainment devices like iPods and Xbox game systems were on every kid's Christmas list. By late 2006 young people typically had at least three different gadgets they used frequently: a phone (for texting), a computer (for social media), and an iPod or game system.

It's almost funny that it took until 2007 for someone to figure out that one device could combine all these platforms. . .and it was the same person responsible for making home computers so user friendly and commonplace.

In January 2007 a man wearing jeans and white sneakers stood on a stage and introduced a device that literally changed the world. His name was Steve Jobs, and his words proved to be prophetic.[7]

"Today Apple is going to reinvent the phone," he said. He described it as a widescreen iPod with touch controls, a revolutionary mobile phone, and a breakthrough internet communications device—all in one.

And America loved it: phone, entertainment, internet, and communications all in one device.

First, Mom and Dad got the iPhone. But once the iPhone 3G came out in 2008, they got the new one and gave their old phone to their kids. Before we knew it, kids began owning iPhones.

Meanwhile, Android released its first smartphone, the G1, with a slide-out keyboard, in 2008. By February 2010 Android released a phone with full touchscreen capability and features that looked just like those of the iPhone. . .which is why in March 2010 Steve Jobs confronted Google chief executive Eric Schmidt about copying iPhone features in the Android, just the beginning of a lengthy legal battle between Apple and Android.[8] But America didn't care, they just kept gobbling up every new gadget that Apple and Samsung would deliver.

In 2010 kids who didn't have the iPhone would borrow Mom or Dad's iPhone to play Angry Birds, dreaming of having their own smartphone someday. Parents kept buying more, and gradually their kids got more. It's no wonder that by 2012 over half of mobile phones in America were smartphones.

In March 2012 Pew Research reported only 23 percent of twelve- to seventeen-year-olds owned smartphones (a report reflecting 2011 numbers).[9] That means at that time the majority of social media was still viewed by teens on a bigger screen plugged into a wall. But that would end soon.

Fast-forward to 2015. Pew Research released a new study revealing that 73 percent of twelve- to seventeen-year-olds had or had access to a smartphone. Their favorite social media platforms were now mobile (Facebook, Instagram, and Snapchat the top three).[10]

By 2018 the average age a kid got their first smartphone was 10.3 years old,[11] and 97% of teens were using social media.[12] And what were the first two apps young people wanted? Snapchat and

Instagram. (Studies show they also use Facebook, but teenagers see that more as a site Mom and Dad use.)

Social media was now in their pocket.

A running meter of how many friends they had was in their pocket.

Every post drew instant feedback in their pocket.

Am I liked? I'd better check the device in my pocket.

Surprise, surprise, by 2018 almost every study on anxiety, depression, and teen suicide cited the smartphone as a key factor.

Why?

That's the question everyone is asking.

LIKE ME

Who doesn't want to be liked?

We now live in a world where the overwhelming majority of young people carry a device in their pockets constantly reminding them exactly where they rank at any moment compared to everybody else.

Think about it. When kids post a picture of their dog, Jake, sleeping upside down on the couch, within minutes they'll know exactly how many people "like" the picture, a number that can easily be compared not only to other pictures they've posted but also to the pictures all their friends have posted. Not to mention, their "friends" or "followers" are also represented by a number—and young people know exactly what that number is, because that number equals *value* today.

How many "friends" do you have?

How many "likes" do you have?

Our kids live in a world where popularity is represented by a number, and almost every post they create is judged, critiqued, and measured.

I don't want to go into too much detail, but a growing number of studies have emerged on this

OUR KIDS LIVE IN A WORLD WHERE POPULARITY IS REPRESENTED BY A NUMBER, AND ALMOST EVERY POST THEY CREATE IS JUDGED, CRITIQUED, AND MEASURED.

subject revealing some eye-opening realities, like kids sitting and watching for "likes" in real time after posting something, or removing posts that don't garner enough "likes."

It's all about the likes!

We might be bewildered by this new phenomenon. . .but young people don't know any different.

One of the wellness counselors I interviewed explained, "To us mean comments on social media might be 'bullying,' but to them it's just a whole different version of being popular. Being liked is a lot of work."

Young people today are experiencing the life of a '90s celebrity. Everywhere they went, these celebrities were followed by multiple sets of eyes judging them on their appearance, their day-to-day activities, even their offhand comments. All were subject to criticism.

Now, everyone lives in that world. They've opted into that world.

As a result, cyberbullying is becoming a blurry line. Is it really cyberbullying, or was that kid just being a little rude?

"I was just being real!"

"Just saying!"

Our culture celebrates rude.

Consider the concept of "diss tracks" in hip-hop culture, songs written with the intention of "dissing" or disrespecting people. Artists most young people treasure, like Kendrick Lamar, Eminem, Jay-Z, and 2Pac are famous for their diss tracks laying waste to other big-name rappers.[13]

So why not "lay waste" to other kids at school if we don't like them?

And what better place to "throw shade" than on social media?

Sadly, cyberbullying is so pervasive, it has become the norm. Whenever someone posts a YouTube video garnering heavy traffic, criticism is unavoidable.

"You sound like a dying whale."

"I can do better."

"WTF!"

"I wanna mute this."

People are mean in the comment section. It's like they can't help it. Maybe it's because they're hiding behind a screen name and don't have the guts to say it face to face.

It happens quite often today. It did with Emily, a junior in high school I interviewed who had become the target of a group of "mean girls" at school. They wrote things on her locker and shouted things from across the hallway, never having the guts to confront her face to face. Then Emily would get pinged on social media from anonymous sources saying, "Yeah, that was me today!"

ANONYMITY

Anonymity always breeds lack of accountability.

Anonymous apps are commonly marketed as a place where you can be "honest"—which really translates "aggressively cruel." These apps allow young people to give anonymous and unmoderated feedback (never a good combination) to other users. Picture a high school locker room where all the bullies wear masks and the coach is nowhere to be found.

Young people are attracted to anonymity in the online world since it allows them to be whoever they want to be. This draws people with low self-esteem because it feels safer than face-to-face communication. They can enter more guarded and present themselves as however they'd like to be seen. Sadly, these anonymous havens are typically rampant with bullies.

Common Sense Media warns parents, "Anonymous apps are notorious hubs for cyberbullying because kids feel emboldened to say things they wouldn't normally."[14] The Common Sense website offers all kinds of current examples of these apps, so I won't date this book by including any in print, but you'll see all kinds of popular platforms claiming they're a fun place to share honest thoughts, when more often they're just online hideouts where kids can say mean things that they're too scared to say to someone's face.

Parents who engage their kids in conversations about the apps they download can help their kids steer clear of these dangerous playgrounds where mockers and intimidators run free.

SEND NUDES. . .OR ELSE

As social media grows more prevalent, intimidation is becoming increasingly more common. Like the eighth-grade girl who had two different guys send her pictures of their penises, "which she did not want and had never asked for."[15] They asked her to reciprocate—sending a nude of herself—and she refused.

Unfortunately, the story doesn't end there. Guys are persistent, and in this situation, she eventually gave in to another boy's request—a boy she liked. Once she sent it, he threatened to post the picture to social media if she didn't send more.

This young girl is not alone. In fact, she's merely feeling the same pressure that countless girls across the world are feeling from guys who are coercing girls to send naked photos, even threatening them if they don't. Researchers from Northwestern University studied 462 stories posted to an anonymous website by twelve- to eighteen-year-old girls. In most of the stories, girls reported persistent pressure to send nudes, where saying no rarely stopped the requests. Many refusals were met with repeated requests, anger, and even threats. Sadly, most of the girls didn't know where to turn. As the report details: "Alternative tactics were largely absent from young women's stories, indicating that young women do not have tools to successfully navigate the challenges they face."[16]

The UK is experiencing similar issues, citing Instagram as one of the worst apps for cyberbullying. A survey of over ten thousand young people ages twelve to twenty discovered 42 percent had experienced cyberbullying on Instagram, and 37 percent on Facebook. The survey also discovered a disconnect between real life and online behavior. "Almost half (47 percent) said they don't discuss bad things in their lives on social media, and instead prefer to present an edited version of themselves."[17]

Young people are attracted to the opportunity to customize a "perfected" version of their online selves. If they find real conversation difficult, they can spend as much time as needed refining the perfect response in digital communication or posting the perfect picture. What young people don't consider is the permanence of what they post. One momentary lapse in judgment, one offhand comment, one weak instance where they post a vulnerable pic, and it's out there for good.

Experts are becoming more vocal about the role social media is playing in causing teen anxiety. Dr. Logan Levkoff, expert in parent-child communication, believes social media is creating a constant pressure for teens. "The challenge with social media is that it doesn't give a young person freedom to make mistakes without being defined by them," Dr. Levkoff explained to ABC News.[18] Many kids feel like they are criticized on social media for almost everything they do.

Sometimes this criticism proves to be too much.

Two freshmen girls in Missouri were invited to a house party thrown by a senior. Fourteen-year-old Daisy was given a glass of alcohol. . .and then another. The next morning Daisy's mother found her crying alone in freezing temperatures on the front lawn. A doctor discovered vaginal tearing. Daisy's friend attested that she was forced to have sex despite saying no countless times.[19]

The town rallied behind the football players and began attacking Daisy on social media. Schoolmates began threatening her, tweeting that she would "get what's coming." They called her a liar and a skank.

The charges were mysteriously dropped, despite the evidence, like numerous witnesses who recalled seeing older boys carrying Daisy out of the house crying. The family eventually moved to avoid harassment.

Two years later in her new town, Daisy went to a party with some friends. That night people began attacking her on Facebook, saying she was a hypocrite and fake for going to a party. They began calling her a slut, claiming that she "wanted it." The onslaughts continued through the weekend.

That Sunday night she attempted to take her own life.[20]

Cyberbullying's reach extends further than any other type of cruelty and intimidation. It makes kids feel like no place is safe.

So what is the best defense against this threat?

CYBERBULLYING'S REACH EXTENDS FURTHER THAN ANY OTHER TYPE OF CRUELTY AND INTIMIDATION. IT MAKES KIDS FEEL LIKE NO PLACE IS SAFE.

DISCUSSION QUESTIONS

1. What was one thing in this chapter that really stood out to you?

2. Which part of the "history of social media" brought back the most memories for you?

3. Countless experts blame the smartphone as at least a contributor to the rise in teen anxiety, depression, and suicide. Do you agree? Explain.

4. Why do you think kids who are cyberbullied are more likely to attempt suicide?

5. Why are people so blunt and rude on social media, especially on anonymous sites?

6. Why do so many girls give in to guys' requests to "send nudes"?

7. How can parents create a "safe place" for their kids in a world where bullying's reach extends further than any other cruelty and intimidation?

CHAPTER 4
THE ESCAPE KEY
Three practices that help prevent cyberbullying

If you're horrible to me, I'm going to write a song about it,
and you won't like it. That's how I operate.
–Taylor Swift

Mallory Grossman was a cheerleader and talented gymnast living in Rockaway, New Jersey, with her mom, dad, and three siblings. Most people described her as happy and lively. . .

Until she took her own life.

It began back in sixth grade when Mallory's life took an unexpected turn. A group of girls at school singled her out and began teasing her.

Her parents don't have any idea what provoked the initial teasing, but it began in the classroom with other students kicking her chair and whispering cruel names like "fat" and "ugly" so the teacher couldn't hear. What might have been labeled teasing grew to shunning. Her fellow students shooed her away if she tried to sit at their lunch table, telling her she didn't have any friends and calling her a loser.[1]

The bullying quickly went digital.

HOME USED TO BE A SANCTUARY, BUT NOW BULLYING REACHES WHEREVER KIDS BRING THEIR PHONES—*WHICH IS EVERYWHERE.*

Cyberbullying is a unique kind of cruelty, because it infiltrates environments that used to feel safe. Home used to be a sanctuary, but now bullying reaches wherever kids bring their phones—*which is everywhere.*

Mallory received cruel texts and posts on Instagram and Snapchat. Girls even posted pictures of Mallory on the playground with mean captions. On one occasion Mallory asked a girl to take a picture down. The girl responded, "NEVER," with a smiley face.

These girls were a unique kind of mean. Mallory's parents heard from other parents who described the girls who bullied Mallory as "mean, malicious, and nasty."

Mallory's mom says she sent countless messages to school officials and they would simply reply, "We'll look into it." But nothing changed.

That's when her parents began noticing symptoms. Mallory's grades began to slip. She would claim she had stomachaches and headaches and needed to stay home from school. "She was just sad," her mother explained.

Mallory's mom spoke to one of the mean girl's mothers. The mother dismissed the accusation that her daughter was bullying, claiming it was all a "big joke" and she shouldn't worry about it. Mallory's mom asked that she please tell her daughter to stop texting Mallory. Mallory received texts from the girl three minutes later.

The parents finally met with the principal and asked the administration to intervene, but felt like the school did not take the claims seriously, even after "months of relentless" cyberbullying. At one meeting her mother said the administration advised Mallory to just "hug it out" with the bullies, and she was actually called out for being a tattletale.[2]

Mallory didn't think telling the school would help. In fact, she told her parents, "You just made it worse. You don't know these girls!" (Words I've heard far too many times from harassed kids.)

Mallory was right. After the meeting, the girls followed her into the bathroom and told her, "If you do that again, we're going to get you."

One kid told Mallory she should just kill herself.

So that's what she did.

She was just twelve years old.

Twelve!

How many times do we have to hear the same story?

Did no one see the signs?

It's interesting hearing today's young people talk about social media. Most of them seem to have a love/hate relationship with it.

In my interviews with kids, I heard phrases like. . .

- "I can't go twenty minutes without it, but then it makes me feel bad about myself when I look at it."
- "Sometimes I know if I post a certain picture I'm going to get made fun of, but I post it anyway."
- "My mom told me to ignore the comments people make, but I can't. They always hurt."

Digital communication has opened up entire new avenues for hurt. How can we possibly help our kids avoid some of this hurt?

DELAY SOCIAL MEDIA AND MOBILE DEVICES

The most effective solution is one more obvious and overlooked than the emperor's new clothes: *delay social media.*

It's like the old joke:

> "Doctor, it hurts when I do this!" The man rotated his arm in a circle.
> "So don't do this!" the doctor replied, rotating his arm in a circle.

Why subject your kids to ridicule on social media when many of them *shouldn't even be* on social media? (I'm specifically referring to kids middle school age and younger.)

In a world where the average kid is getting a smartphone at ten years old, and devices with all the same features at even younger ages, we need to ask ourselves, "Are we helping or hindering our kids by handing them these devices?"

Yes, cyberbullying is difficult enough for thirteen-year-olds, fifteen-year-olds, and seventeen-year-olds. We don't need to subject our eleven- and twelve-year-olds to it. In fact, the government forbids it.

I'm talking about COPPA, the Federal Trade Commission's "Children's Online Privacy Protection Act," which prevents websites and online services (like Snapchat, Instagram, and Twitter) from collecting personal information from anyone under thirteen.

What does that mean?

When your twelve-year-old tries to sign up for Snapchat, the first thing the app does is ask them to enter their birthdate. If they are under thirteen, then Snapchat basically says, "Sorry, you're not old enough." Same with Instagram and Twitter.

So why are countless ten-, eleven-, and twelve-year-olds on social media?

Because they lied about their age.

That's the frustrating element. The FTC has no way to enforce the age rule, and apps don't require any sort of age verification. As a result, even if you don't allow your twelve-year-old to have Snapchat, many of their friends will have Snapchat (or as your child will tell you, "*All* my friends have Snapchat").

SO WHY ARE COUNTLESS TEN-, ELEVEN-, AND TWELVE-YEAR-OLDS ON SOCIAL MEDIA? BECAUSE THEY LIED ABOUT THEIR AGE.

And they're right. Sadly, most young people are on social media. In fact, studies reveal that three out of five young people had their first social media account at age twelve or under.[3]

That probably explains why you've read so many stories about eleven- and twelve-year-olds being targeted and ridiculed on social media. Almost every story includes something about them being attacked on Snapchat, Instagram, or Facebook when they weren't even supposed to be on Snapchat, Instagram, or Facebook. Laws and use policies combined mean your children are prohibited from using them without your consent. The FTC forbids it.

So when should we allow our kids to be on social media?

Health experts agree that parents should delay social media as long as possible. In fact, in January 2018, "a coalition of 97 child health advocates sent a letter to Mark Zuckerberg asking him to discontinue Messenger Kids, a new advertising-free Facebook app targeted at 6- to 12-year olds." The letter said, "Raising children in our new digital age is difficult enough. We ask that you do not use Facebook's enormous reach and influence to make it even harder."[4] One of those who signed the letter was San Diego State University professor Jean Twenge, author of *iGen*.

I had the opportunity to talk with Dr. Twenge at a conference where she presented compelling data showing a huge spike in teen depression, suicide, and overall "unhappiness" in the last five years— just after America crossed the 50 percent mark for smartphone ownership. She highlighted numerous studies showing a correlation between social media and "unhappiness." One study randomly assigned participants to give up Facebook for a week. Those who did reported feeling less depressed.[5]

I asked her why she signed the letter asking Zuckerberg to stop targeting six- to twelve-year-olds with social media. Her answer was simple: "Because they're just kids!"

But cyberbullying isn't limited to social media. Texting is another common tool for cyberbullies.

Do you know the best way to prevent your twelve-year-old from getting mean texts?

Delay giving them a mobile device.

Don't take it from me. Again, listen to the health experts. For example, Jim Steyer, CEO of Common Sense Media, was asked when he recommended allowing a young person to get a smartphone. At first Jim didn't give a number. He gave politically correct answers like, "No two kids are the same, so it's hard to name one age for all kids."

But the press continued to ask. "When? Give us an age!"

Jim said, "The longer you wait, the better."

Finally someone asked him, "When did you give your kids smartphones?"

Jim responded, "When they were in high school and they learned responsibility."[6]

Bill Gates, CEO of Microsoft, was asked the same question. You'd think Bill's kids would have had smartphones coming out of the womb, right?

Wrong.

Bill didn't let any of his three kids have a smartphone until they were fourteen and they were in high school.[7]

Think of all the drama you can avoid by delaying social media and mobile devices until high school. And once your kids get to the age where you think they're responsible enough to get a device, educate them first. Note I said "delay," not "forbid." We need to teach our kids how to use social media responsibly. If you feel ill-equipped to do this, just use a resource like my book *The Teen's Guide to Social Media and Mobile Devices* as a phone contract. "When we're done reading this book together, you can have a device." Meet with them each week and go through the discussion questions at the end of each chapter, opening up the doors of dialogue about important issues like what they're posting, who they're "friending," and safety precautions like whether they are allowing their location to be seen in features like "Snap Maps."

Delaying social media can delay a lot of grief.

I can't even begin to tell you how many parents approach me at my parent workshops sharing nightmares about their tweens on social media, or conversations these kids had with some boy or girl late at night. Which brings me to my next tip. . .

DELAYING SOCIAL MEDIA CAN DELAY A LOT OF GRIEF.

KEEP DEVICES OUT OF BEDROOMS

Way back in 2010 the American Academy of Pediatrics (AAP) told parents it wasn't a good idea for kids to have TV or internet in their bedrooms. Of course, this was before the majority of young people had TV and internet on a device they kept in their pocket. But now that the overwhelming majority of teens have a smartphone in their pocket, with complete access to social media. . .the AAP has not changed its stance. Not only does the AAP recommend that kids not sleep with devices in their bedroom; it also advises avoiding exposure to screens for one hour before bedtime, since that can disrupt sleep.[8]

Think how many social media rants and mean comments would be prevented if all parents followed this advice.

Sadly, a poll conducted in the United States by the National Sleep Foundation revealed that 89 percent of teens have at least one device in their sleep environment that negatively influences their sleep.[9]

Today's kids have very few safe zones. Wouldn't it be nice if the bedroom was a sanctuary where they were safe from bullying? Or even if from 8:00 p.m. on it was a tech-free zone?

The *Journal of Youth Studies* conducted a study surveying over nine hundred adolescents between twelve and fifteen years old and discovered that one in five reported "almost always" waking up to check social media or text messages throughout the night. Those who did check their phones not only were three times more likely to report feeling "consistently tired" at school, but "reported significantly lower levels of wellbeing than their classmates."[10]

Don't get me wrong; I'm not suggesting that if our kids don't have devices in their bedrooms, they will be immune from bullying. Bullies can still say mean things during the day. But we can limit the influence of bullies by limiting their reach. There is no reason your kids need to be inundated with the regular pings of bullies throughout the night.

It's amazing how much bullying goes on at night. Google the words "late-night cyberbullying" and you'll discover countless stories about people receiving late-night hate texts or seeing late-night mean posts or comments, all when young people are in their rooms alone with no accountability at all.

And mean words aren't the only things young people end up viewing when they have their device in their room late at night. In a world rampant with porn, young people are soaking in plenty of it. . .even very young. Sadly, one in ten visitors to graphic porn sites are under ten years old.[11]

What does this have to do with bullying or intimidation? The connection is closer than you might think. Consider this study highlighted in the cover article of *Time* magazine:

> In a study of behaviors in popular porn, nearly 90%

of 304 random scenes contained physical aggression toward women, who nearly always responded neutrally or with pleasure. More insidiously, women would sometimes beg their partners to stop, then acquiesce and begin to enjoy the activity, regardless of how painful or debasing.[12]

No wonder girls are receiving countless messages and texts asking them to send nude pics. Because they all must "want it," right?

These pressures and intimidations are bad enough during the day. Our kids don't need to be experiencing them all night. Do your kids a favor and plug their phones into a charger in your bedroom every night an hour before bedtime. Who knows? This practice might encourage some actual face-to-face conversation, which leads to my next point. . .

MAXIMIZE FACE-TO-FACE INTERACTION

Consider what we've discussed in this chapter alone. The more someone is on social media, the more unhappy they are. In fact, the more time a young person spends online, the more likely they will experience mental health issues. "Teens who spent five or more hours a day online were 71 percent more likely than those who spent only one hour a day to have at least one suicide risk factor (depression, thinking about suicide, making a suicide plan, or attempting suicide)." The one antidote health and wellness experts seem to agree on is face-to-face interaction. Dr. Jean Twenge argues, "Interacting with people face to face is one of the deepest wellsprings of human happiness."[13]

So consistently look for opportunities to interact with your kids, and encourage them to get involved in hobbies, sports, and social events where they interact with others.

But begin in the home. Bullying makes young people feel worthless, helpless, humiliated, and socially isolated. Make home a place where they feel exactly the opposite. Make them feel valued, empowered, honored, and an important part of the family. Find settings where your kids relax and open up. You might have to be proactive and look for venues they enjoy. Take them out for french fries at a restaurant they like, or join them in playing their favorite video game. These fun settings often catalyze moments of meaningful conversation. Don't force conversation; just seek out times of face-to-face interaction and conversation will eventually happen naturally.

One of the simplest venues I suggest in my book *52 Ways to Connect with Your Smartphone-Obsessed Kid* is dinnertime. I merely advised families to try "no tech at the table"—that includes Mom and Dad. Make dinner a cherished time when screens are turned off and phones set aside for even just half an hour. This doesn't guarantee meaningful conversation every meal, but it does open the door to dialogue. Some of my best conversations with my kids were at the family dinner table.

Maximize every opportunity to connect with your child.

FOOLPROOF

It would be foolish for me to say that these three steps I've shared will completely prevent cyberbullying and bullying. Sadly, a loving home and a few prudent guardrails aren't a bulletproof vest. I've met countless parents—really good parents—who made all the right efforts and their child still suffered ridicule. I know a mom and dad who signed up their son for football so he could meet new friends and boost his confidence, only to find the football field another place where he was mocked for not being good enough.

Sometimes "prevention" isn't foolproof. Some kids just have a more difficult time making friends. And when teased, many are ignorant of the conflict management skills that can help them evade recurring incidents.

So how can a caring adult offer ongoing support?

It all begins with being approachable. Let's focus on what that looks like in the next chapter.

DISCUSSION QUESTIONS

1. What was one thing in this chapter that really stood out to you?

2. Why do you think young people spend time on social media even if it's frequently a painful place for them?

3. Why are so many kids under age thirteen on social media sites that forbid anyone under thirteen?

4. How should a caring parent respond to their twelve-year-old who asks, "Can I have Snapchat?"

5. Why do you think Bill Gates, Jim Steyer, and other experts on the world of technology make their kids wait until high school to get a smartphone?

6. How would life change if every young person turned off their phone at bedtime and put it on a charger in their parents' bedroom?

7. Why do you think Dr. Jean Twenge claims, "Interacting with people face to face is one of the deepest wellsprings of human happiness"?

8. What is one way you could implement one of the three practices covered in this chapter with a young person this week?

CHAPTER 5
"WHY DIDN'T YOU SAY ANYTHING?"
Avoiding the rush to blame

"What do you mean he hit you?
Why? What did you do
to provoke him?"

. . . And we wonder why our kids don't come to us.

When I was in fourth grade, back when kids actually walked home from school, my brother and I got jumped on our way home.

Earlier that day, Sam, one of my classmates, stole my journal. My journal was a big deal—at least it was to my teacher, Mrs. Sumpel, who wanted us to write in it daily. Sam didn't want to write in his journal, so he stole mine, erased my name from the top of every page, and wrote his name in its place (not a brilliant scheme by any means). I reported it to the teacher at the end of the day, and Sam denied it. The journal was nowhere to be found, so she said we'd deal with it the next day.

After school Sam and his brothers waited until my brother and I were halfway home and began picking a fight. They shoved me to the ground, pulled out a knife, and threatened us, but somehow my brother and I managed to flee.

I was terrified. I didn't want to walk to school the next day. But my brother convinced me that we'd never be allowed to go anywhere on our own again if we told Mom and Dad. "Mom will freak!"

So we opted not to tell anyone.

The next day something surprising happened. When I arrived at school, Mrs. Sumpel was irate. She grabbed me by the shoulder and dragged me into the hallway. Sam was in the hallway crying (he was a far better actor than he was a criminal).

Mrs. Sumpel was fuming. She wagged her finger at me. "You are going to get some swats for this!" (Some of you remember the days when schools could spank. She had a big paddle hanging on her wall.)

She turned to Sam and in a soft voice asked, "Tell us what happened."

Sam sniffed and wiped his tears. Finally he managed to point at me. "He stole my journal and said it was his." He held up *my journal*.

Mrs. Sumpel shot her stare back toward me. "That's one swat!"

Before I could object, Sam continued his Oscar-winning performance. "And then he and his brother cornered me after school. . ."

I was shocked. This kid was living in a house of lies!

Mrs. Sumpel turned to me once again. "That's another swat!" She was livid. I think steam was actually leaking out of her ears.

Sam continued, "And then they shoved me on the ground. . ."

"And that's another one!" Mrs. Sumpel said, frothing at the mouth.

"Wait," I finally managed to interject. "Don't you wanna hear my side of the story?"

Mrs. Sumpel reluctantly agreed.

"First," I said, pointing to the journal, "that's my journal. Take a look for yourself."

Mrs. Sumpel hesitantly asked Sam, "Can I see the journal?"

Sam handed her the journal, and she began investigating every page. The name Jonathan was poorly erased on every page, clearly still legible, and the name Sam was scratched over it. As she flipped through the pages, her expression changed.

After a few moments, once she realized the major flaw in Sam's story, I told her the true version.

With no apology, she quietly told me, "Okay, you can go."

This experience cemented two things in my mind.

1. Mrs. Sumpel was straight-up crazy.
2. Teachers can't be trusted.

The next year I experienced a similar occurrence with a teacher. I walked into the boys' bathroom to find three or four older boys kicking the flush handles. One boy had done his best karate kick to flush the handle (which is actually a pretty sanitary way to flush if you think about it), and the other boys followed suit. I hadn't even used the toilet yet when the principal barged in and herded all of us out into the hallway.

He lined us all up and went to his office to fetch his paddle. It had holes in it for less wind resistance and a harder smack. We called it "the whistler." It had a very unique tone compared to the other paddles in the school.

"You guys were hurting school property!" he barked.

I spoke up. "Not me! I wasn't even—"

"Quiet!" He wasn't having any of it. We were all declared guilty without trial. He simply asked, "Who's first?"

I can still remember the sound it made.

It didn't take me long to realize, *Adults frequently get it wrong.*

SILENCE

"Why didn't you say anything?"

The most common words adults use when they discover a young person has been bullied.

If only kids would answer honestly.

"Because I don't trust you."

"Because I knew you'd make the situation worse."

"Because you're just going to tell me it's my fault."

My guess is that the school down the street from you has made some antibullying efforts. A school assembly. Posters in classrooms. Maybe even a policy that they are intolerant of bullying.

But are these broad gestures helping?

Do young people feel safe to speak up?

The US Department of Education conducted a recent study about victimization in which they asked over 24 million kids about bullying. That's a lot of kids. In the study a little over 20 percent of sixth through twelfth graders said they had been bullied. . .yet less than half of those told an adult.

Sixth graders were most likely to tell an adult—over 60 percent of bullied kids said something. But by high school those numbers go way down, with only 35 percent of bullied freshmen reporting what happened, and only 26 percent of bullied seniors.[1]

I asked about a dozen of the teachers I interviewed how many incidents of bullying were reported at their schools. The average answer reflected less than 10 percent of students.

Less than 10 percent?

We've already looked at studies in this book revealing that anywhere from 20 to 50 percent of kids experience bullying on any given campus. Why are less than 10 percent of kids reporting bullying?

Why aren't kids speaking up?

More importantly, how can a caring adult create a climate where kids feel safe to talk about being targeted?

WHY AREN'T KIDS SPEAKING UP?

RUSH TO BLAME

It's never easy being a parent or teacher charged with the task of discipline—especially when there are different stories. When teachers experience a verbal exchange or disruption in the classroom, no buzzer goes off to alert them it's a bullying situation.

It happens to parents all the time. We hear our kids raising their voices and know we should intervene. We're like the Terminator seeing possible responses scrolling on our digital display:

1. "Knock it off!"
2. "What's going on in there?"
3. "You two had better start getting along, or you've got another thing coming!"

If the fighting gets worse, we actually have to put down what we're doing and go play cop or arbitrator. If they're lucky, they'll get the latter.

"Okay, someone tell me what happened."

Then the stories begin.

"I was playing a video game and Michael came in and turned it off."

"No, I didn't! Chris was hogging the video games all day, and whenever I asked if I could play, he said, 'You snooze, you lose!' "

"Did not!"

"Did so!"

Now it's our job to find out what really happened, which often is the fault of both parties. That's why we sometimes rush to the judgment.

"Well then, *no one* gets to play!"

Which is why most younger siblings opt *not* to tell on their sibling, because they know they'll get in trouble too, regardless of innocence! (I'm speaking for all younger siblings!)

Sure, kids can experience bullying of sorts by an older sibling, but typically it's just a selfish sibling exerting power control for their own self-seeking reasons. When it's two random kids at school, the situation becomes all the more difficult.

The powerful documentary *Bully*[2] includes a sobering scene where a principal catches two kids quarreling and makes the boys shake hands. One kid quickly complies, politely offering his hand. The other refuses to shake hands. The principal immediately scolds the kid who doesn't offer his hand.

The scene was difficult for me to watch, as a kid who was picked on daily. In fact, many who have reviewed the film have commented something like, "I was screaming at the screen watching these stupid teachers and principals!"

The scene was frustrating to watch because we—the viewing audience—had a huge advantage over the principal: perspective. We had just spent the entire movie watching one kid make this other kid's life miserable, taunting him and pushing him while other kids laughed. The principal caught the tail end of one of these interactions, seeing two boys not getting along, and tried to solve the problem quickly.

"You guys shake hands."

This was an absurd effort at peacekeeping on several levels. First, what has handshaking ever solved? Someone please show me some data revealing that shaking hands calms tempers, erases wrongs, and promotes peace and harmony.

There is no such data.

Second, the principal rushed to a resolution. Schoolteachers and administrators have so much on their plates, they often don't have the time it takes to truly listen to both sides of a story. So sometimes they try shortcuts to a quick resolution.

"Both of you quit it, or you'll both be sorry."

Maybe a threat like this will stop the bickering temporarily, but it rarely stops the problem. If feelings were hurt, they typically don't heal themselves. The conflict usually resumes later exactly where it left off.

SCHOOLTEACHERS AND ADMINISTRATORS HAVE SO MUCH ON THEIR PLATES, THEY OFTEN DON'T HAVE THE TIME IT TAKES TO TRULY LISTEN TO BOTH SIDES OF A STORY. SO SOMETIMES THEY TRY SHORTCUTS TO A QUICK RESOLUTION.

In the documentary, the poor bullied kid refused to shake hands. He wasn't about to shake the hand of the snake whose venomous daily attacks had left him feeling worthless and hopeless. The principal responded by shaming the kid who wouldn't extend his hand. In fact, she dismissed the bully and began reprimanding the bullied.

"He was willing to shake your hand. It was *you* who wouldn't shake hands."

At this point the victim realized it wasn't just kids but also adults who were against him.

We should note, however, that apparently when the principal eventually saw the film and gained perspective on the entire situation, she felt terrible and signed off on the filmmakers showing this embarrassing scene because she thought it would help other principals avoid making the same mistake.

So how can we gain a big-picture perspective and avoid making mistakes like this? In other words, how can a parent, teacher, or any authority figure spot the signs of bullying and not rush to blame?

RUSH

Here's a phrase parents hear from me a lot at my parent seminars: "Parenting is a lot of work."

It takes work to notice what's going on in the world of our kids, it takes work to be proactive about connecting with our kids, it takes work to truly listen to our kids, and yes, it takes work to uncover the truth in a disagreement between two kids.

Who has time for all this work?

The temptation is to rush through some of it.

But that doesn't work.

In my research for my book *If I Had a Parenting Do-over*, I asked hundreds of parents just one question: "If you could go back in time and change one parenting practice, what would you do over?"

One answer kept emerging. It was the most common answer by a landslide.

"I wish I'd spent more time with my kids."

The answer came in many forms: "I wish we would have had more family meals." Or "I wish I would have actually walked into my kids' room, sat down on the floor, and talked with them while they were doing their homework."

But the gist was clear. They wish they would have devoted the time to connect with their kids.

You can't rush through parenting, and you certainly can't rush through getting to the bottom of a story.

Realize that getting to the truth takes time. If you're a teacher and don't have time to stop teaching thirty kids to deal with two, then send the two kids to someone who *can* spend the time. Schools need to be set up that way. Every kid should get a fair shot. No kid should be declared guilty when they only received a seven-second trial (more on this in chapter eleven).

Eliminate any rush to judgment.

Eliminate the rush to blame.

NO KID SHOULD BE DECLARED GUILTY WHEN THEY ONLY RECEIVED A SEVEN-SECOND TRIAL

BLAME

Hindsight is 20/20. If we could watch a movie and see the entire story, it would be much easier to avoid blaming the innocent—blaming the bullied.

But it happens all the time. It's almost automatic. It's why rape victims often don't come forward. They know what responses they'll hear.

- "Were you drinking?"
- "Did you lead him on?"
- "Did you actually say no?"
- "Why did you wait until now to say anything?"

Rape victims don't want to come forward because they know they will be put on trial. The victim automatically becomes a suspect.

The same is true with bullying.

- "Are you sure that happened?"
- "Maybe he was just joking."
- "Well, what did you do to make him so mad?"
- "Have you tried just ignoring him?"

How can we expect victims of bullying to ask for help when they know they will be interrogated?

How can we avoid rushing to blame?

The key is in resisting the need to "fix" the situation. Personally, I struggle with this because I am a fixer! But bullied kids aren't typically ready to be fixed. Most of the time they just want to be noticed and heard.

That's where we need to start.

DISCUSSION QUESTIONS

1. What was one thing in this chapter that really stood out to you?

2. Why do you think most bullying victims don't report bullying?

3. Why do you think most bystanders don't report bullying?

4. What are some ways you might "rush" through parenting when it comes to either connecting with your kids or just getting to the bottom of a story?

5. What are some common ways we might unintentionally "blame" kids who are bullied?

6. Do you tend to want to "fix" your child's problems right away, or stop to notice and hear? How does that typically work out for you?

7. What is something you can try this week to avoid rushing to blame?

CHAPTER 6
I'M RIGHT HERE
Three practices helping us notice and hear

The most important thing in communication
is hearing what isn't said.
–Peter Drucker

If only I had a dime for every time I've heard a parent say, "I had no idea."

The divide only seems to have grown with the increasing use of social media and mobile devices. Kids are isolating themselves more and more, spending more screen time than face time, and as a result moms and dads know less and less about what's actually going on in the lives of their kids.

Teachers, administrators, and chaperones are experiencing the same disconnect. It doesn't matter if they share the same classrooms and hallways each day. Mere proximity doesn't create familiarity. We need adults who care enough to *notice*.

An adult presence doesn't prevent bullying; it just relocates it. Don't get me wrong—I'm a huge advocate for adult presence, especially in places that seem void of supervision, like hallways and locker rooms. But we don't need two adult chaperones standing together out on a playground talking with each other. We need adults who interact with kids.

AN ADULT PRESENCE DOESN'T PREVENT BULLYING; IT JUST RELOCATES IT.

Why don't adults do this?

It's a question we discuss frequently in youth ministry circles. Adults tend to migrate together and talk about work or their kids' sports instead of mingling with kids. It's difficult for some adults to detach from the comfort of adult conversation and engage a young person in conversation.

Parents have the same struggle. Let's be honest. Juvenile conversation is often. . .juvenile. Yet today's young people need adults who are willing to seek them out and show an interest *in their world*. Honestly, most young people have very few adults in their lives who actually do this.

So what does this kind of connection with young people look like?

Here are three practices I've observed that help caring adults create a climate of comfortable conversation for students who are being hurt repeatedly by their peers.

1. USE YOUR EYES AND EARS BEFORE YOUR MOUTH.

Connecting with young people can be difficult, especially when we don't know anything about them. That's why I always advise parents, teachers, pastors, and coaches to use their eyes and ears before their mouths.

You'll be amazed what mere observation will reveal. Kids aren't half as sly as they think they are.

Just watch them.

What are they wearing?

What are they talking about with their friends?

What are they watching and listening to on their phones?

I do this whenever I visit students on campus. Sometimes it takes a little effort. Communication requires putting myself out there (which honestly requires pretty good self-esteem as an adult, because teenagers can be mean).

For me, connecting with new kids means thinking five minutes ahead and having some questions handy that might open up the doors of dialogue. Many of the best questions you can ask begin with noticing. Notice the shoes they're wearing, the T-shirt they chose, if they have headphones on, if they're eating a snack. Any of those elements can be your start to a conversation.

- "I like your shoes. Are those LeBrons?"

- "I like your T-shirt. Do you like Beyoncé or did you just borrow your sister's shirt?"
- "What song are you listening to? Are you listening to an entire album, or a playlist?"
- "Cheetos! Nice. What else is good at the snack bar here?"

Ask these questions openly, as someone truly curious about the answers, not as a parole officer looking for malfeasance. Most adults don't take time to notice today's young people, so don't be surprised if they're a little skeptical of your taking an interest in them.

Parents can experience this skepticism just the same, especially parents of teenagers. If kids are used to being ignored, they might grow suspicious when Mom finally takes an interest in them. The typical conversation in many homes might be, "How was school?"

"Fine."

"Anything exciting happen?"

"Nope."

"Got any homework?"

"Just a little."

Silence.

Here's where moms and dads can try taking notice and looking for something that might actually spark an interest with their kids. Asking "How was your day?" every day gets a little dry. Try observational questions with them. Most young people have something they would love to talk about, but don't have anyone who will listen. Once you discover what that is, they might even talk your ear off.

What are your kids' interests?

What do they get excited about?

What do they laugh about with their friends?

What do they spend most of their money on?

What do they spend most of their time doing?

What video games do they like?

Have you ever played with them?

What music do they like?

Have you ever listened to their playlists?

What movies or Netflix shows do they enjoy?

Have you ever binged a show with them?

Who is their best friend?

What is their favorite activity on a given Friday night?

What is their favorite place to eat?

What do they order?

Notice these things and ask your kids about them and you have higher odds of getting a response.

The reason most adults can't get teens to open up is because they aren't willing to take the time to notice and create that connection. When an adult enters the kid's world, notices something, engages them, and gets them nodding their head or laughing. . .*the connection is made.*

You have to ask yourself, "What would get them nodding, laughing, or talking my ear off?"

Once you take notice of something they enjoy, use questions to begin peeling back layers. If a kid shares about a song she's listening to on a certain playlist, maybe ask her, "What do you call that playlist?" Then you can follow up her response with questions that might peel back a few more layers.

- "When do you typically listen to that playlist?"
- "What playlist do you probably listen to more than any other?"
- "What is your go-to playlist when you're feeling happy?"
- "What is your go-to playlist when you're feeling sad?"
- "Does it help?"
- "What else helps?"

Obviously you have to pace yourself with these questions. Notice I began with light questions like, "What are you listening to?" I didn't start with, "Does that playlist help you when you're sad?" But don't be afraid to take baby steps and peel back some layers. Let them know you're a safe person to talk with.

A mom confessed to me that she was a terrible listener. She felt like it was her own fault that her older kids never opened up to her.

So she made a shift with her youngest daughter, being proactive about dropping everything whenever her daughter entered the room. This mom called it "intentional listening." After a year of disciplined "intentional listening," she said her daughter began completely opening up. Still to this day she says her youngest daughter will talk her ear off.

"I think it's because she became so used to having someone who actually listened," she said.

Moms, dads, teachers, chaperones. . .we all need to be more than just "an adult presence." We aren't going to discover what's going on in the lives of our kids unless we take time to notice them and engage them in meaningful conversation.

Try this today. Set a deadline for yourself of when you're going to talk to a certain kid. Go ahead and set a reminder on your phone. If you know you need to start a conversation with this kid by 7:00 p.m., you'll probably find yourself doing a little recon in the meantime, taking notice of what they're wearing, what they're doing on their phone, who they're talking to, etc. If you see them talking with other friends, you'll probably even take note of what they're talking about, when they laugh, when they get upset. All these observations provide intel you can use to engage them in conversation, and they help increase your awareness of their situation. This process isn't instantaneous. Keep at it. It takes time to peel those layers.

What's more, some kids just aren't as easy to get to know.

2. PROACTIVELY ENGAGE THE AWKWARD AND ALONE.

Sometimes it's easier to talk with bullies than the bullied.

Don't get mad at me for saying it. Trust me, I'm a little offended myself. Remember, I was definitely in the "bullied" category. But the fact remains: sometimes, not always, but sometimes the bullied are bullied because they are socially awkward. (Remember the "downward spiral" on page 24?) So sometimes it's easier for adults to engage in dialogue with popular kids or kids who blend in socially.

This is why bullies sometimes evade getting into trouble. Many bullies are popular for a reason. They're likable. They're socially shrewd, where bullied kids might be difficult. So when the principal catches the two of them in a disagreement, guess who usually wins the principal over? (Think Eddie Haskell, for those of you old enough.)

If you want to open up the doors of dialogue with kids who might be targeted or picked on, then you probably should be taking notice of fringe kids, quiet kids who keep to themselves, or those painfully awkward kids who are really difficult to engage. So surprise them—engage them. Show them unconditional acceptance. Talk with them just like they are anyone else.

This is the embodiment of Jesus' teaching. Some don't even know it's from Him; they just call it the Golden Rule: "Do to others whatever you would like them to do to you" (Matthew 7:12 NLT). Jesus said this in His famous Sermon on the Mount, the same sermon in which He told us to mourn for others, be merciful, love our enemies, be kind to those who aren't our friends, and reconcile any relationships that are hurting.

I'll never forget a very unusual girl named Christina who visited my campus program years ago. This girl was overweight, unkempt, obnoxiously loud, and awkward. The first time I saw her walk into a room, I heard audible groans from the other kids.

When I tried talking with her she actually insulted me, probably a defense mechanism from her own insecurity. She thought if she could beat me to the punch, maybe other kids would laugh.

No one did.

Just a painful silence.

When I met with my adult leaders and asked them who wanted Christina in their small group, everyone was deathly silent. Honestly, I think no one wanted the burden. One kid can really affect a small group negatively. That's why we were all relieved when Jill, one of my new leaders, took a liking to Christina. I still remember the week Jill mentioned wanting to spend some time with Christina. All my other leaders immediately encouraged her, "That's awesome! Go for it." They were glad someone else stepped in to deal with her antics.

Intriguingly, Jill made unprecedented breakthroughs with Christina.

How?

She spent time with her one-on-one. She noticed her interests and asked questions about those interests. In fact, Christina had a pet snake, which horrified Jill. But Jill asked all kinds of questions about snakes, even went to the pet shop with Christina to buy food for the snake (don't make me tell you what "food" they bought). This love and attention opened the floodgates of conversation with Christina.

Within just a few weeks Jill uncovered a Christina no one had met, a very insecure girl hiding behind repugnant defense mechanisms and masks. The real Christina was actually very generous and sweet (unless you were a bunny). Not many people knew this Christina, because they didn't invest the time or patience. Bullied kids can require lots of both.

It all starts with a willingness to seek them out and extend a little understanding, which requires us to. . .

3. EMPATHIZE.

Most bullied kids feel like no one understands or cares. Empathy shows them you do.

Whenever someone is bullied, the typical response is to begin asking a lot of questions to "get to the bottom of it." We want to fix the problem. Resist the temptation to interrogate. Instead just say, "Wow, I'm so sorry you're going through this."

RESIST THE TEMPTATION TO INTERROGATE.

Bullied kids are used to being offered advice. "Have you tried. . ."

Don't tell them what they should do. It's like telling someone depressed to just "be happy." They've tried it. It hasn't worked. And our advice just cements the fact that we don't understand what it's like to be them.

Don't worry—there will be a time for problem-solving and "fixes." But do you know what they need more than solutions right now?

A friend.

So start with a little understanding. Tell yourself that you're going to delay any solutions at the moment. Your goal is connection.

Empathy fuels connection. Empathy makes bullied kids feel like someone is willing to go through this hell with them.

So listen to their perspective and try to see through their eyes.

Don't minimize what they're feeling. Avoid starting any sentence with the words, "At least. . ." Like if your friend had a miscarriage, you wouldn't say, "At least you know you can get pregnant!"

It doesn't help.

Right now their pain feels bigger than life. You aren't seeing through their eyes when you minimize that pain.

Recognize their emotions and communicate with them what you feel.

"It sounds like you feel overwhelmed. I know that feeling. I hate that."

Delay the urge to provide solutions. It's probably better to say, "I don't even know what to say to that; I'm just so glad you told me."

Counselors call this validating. It's basically saying, "You aren't crazy. This stuff hurts. You're normal to feel this way."

If a kid has been to a lot of counseling, they might have heard a lot of "I'm sorry you are going through this." It might even begin to sound trite. If this is the case, use your own words. Don't come across as clinical. If you are genuinely concerned, allow them to see that.

And you don't need to know all the answers. In fact, if they stump you with a question, try using the phrase, "I don't know, but. . ." For example:

- "I don't know, but that's a good question."
- "I don't know, but I've definitely felt that way."
- "I don't know, but you're not alone."
- "I don't know, but thanks for telling me."

They might even ask you a question that you know an answer to, but hold off on giving them an answer right then. First, prove that they have a friend they can trust.

SOMEONE

While surveying hundreds of young people for this book and interviewing dozens of bullying victims, I began hearing a similar cry of hurt. Notice I didn't write "cry for help."

I don't think many of the young people I talked with were ready to ask for help. They actually were *not* seeking solutions.

They were seeking a friend.

I know that feeling. In the midst of my hurt, the greatest need I had was *someone* who knew what I was feeling.

Are you willing to be that individual for a young person out there?

Real help begins with noticing, listening, seeking out, and empathizing. Once those connections are made, the groundwork for healing has been laid.

The question is this: Is that kid you care so much about a bully, a bystander, or the bullied?

DISCUSSION QUESTIONS

1. What was one thing in this chapter that really stood out to you?

2. What did Jonathan mean by "an adult presence doesn't prevent bullying; it just relocates it"?

3. How can schools, churches, and any youth organizations do a better job of finding and equipping adults who are "more than an adult presence" and actually interact with kids?

4. Why does the simple act of "noticing" what music your kids listen to, what shows they watch, who their friends are, what they like to do on Friday night, etc., increase your odds of getting a response from them?

5. What gets your kids laughing, nodding, and talking?

6. Why can it be easier to engage in conversation with *bullies* than with *the bullied*?

7. What is one way you can show empathy to your kids this week?

CHAPTER 7
THE BULLY
In the minds of the bullies. . .and how to actually help them

Bullies are people who use conflict as a means
for obtaining power. Some young people grow
out of this; others don't and become old bullies.
–Bob Goff

Three categories of young people stand out on any given campus today: the bully, the bystander, and the bullied.

Which one were you?

Which one is your kid?

It's an especially uncomfortable reality for parents to think about. One of my daughters looks back at her early years and admits, "I was mean. Honestly, once I got in with the popular kids, it was normal to laugh at those who weren't."

When my wife, Lori, and I first heard her admit that, the first words out of our mouths were, "You weren't really *that* bad, were you?"

Funny, as I rethink my own reaction, I realize it's leaning toward denial. Sure, as a parent you want to support your kid and help them not beat themselves up for their past, but there's also a little bit of, "You didn't really do that, did you?" which might really suggest, "We didn't raise you that way!"

It's hard to think of our own kid as a bully. Trust me, I don't want to be the one pointing the finger at your kid. If there's one thing that makes mama bear mad, it's poking her cubs.

But that's just it. Many moms and dads don't realize what's truly going on in the lives of their "cubs." For teachers it's even more difficult to discern. Many teachers are so overwhelmed with managing a classroom that they don't have time to sort through the drama and discover what's really happening in the lives of their students.

After listening to countless stories from young people in all three groups, as well as observing young people for the last three decades, I've found in most situations the evidence of bullying was obvious to anyone who cared enough to notice and knew what to look for.

So what do each of these kids look like?

Let's spend a little time peeking into the mind-set of individuals in each of these categories: the bully, the bystander, and the bullied.

I'VE FOUND IN MOST SITUATIONS THE EVIDENCE OF BULLYING WAS OBVIOUS TO ANYONE WHO CARED ENOUGH TO NOTICE AND KNEW WHAT TO LOOK FOR.

In this chapter we'll look at the bully.

RUDE, MEAN BULLY

I interviewed a kid I'll call Jake who had a dramatic experience in middle school. He liked a girl I'll call Becca and wanted to ask her to a school dance. So Jake did what any middle school kid does—he asked his friends to ask Becca's friends if she liked him and wanted to go to the dance with him.

The verdict came back "yes," so Jake decided to ask her.

At this particular school, many if not most boys asked girls in a very creative way. They would make a sign and hold it up in the cafeteria or get a friend to announce it over the intercom. Jake was pretty shy, and the thought of attempting a huge public "ask" frightened him. But listening to his sister's advice, he bought a bouquet of flowers and waited in the center hall, a central hub where most kids hung out or at least passed through on the way to lunch, the perfect location to officially ask Becca to the dance. Becca's best friend had class with Becca before lunch and assured Jake that she would be walking through there.

Everything was set.

As Jake stood there waiting, people began whispering and texting. "Jake's going to ask Becca to the dance." The buzzing traveled down the hallway where Becca and her best friend were approaching. People began making comments.

"Becca's gonna go to the dance."

"Watch out. . . Jake's ready to pounce!"

Becca heard the comments and panicked, stopping dead in her tracks. She was only twenty feet from the center hall where Jake was waiting.

"What?" her friend asked.

"I don't know if I want to go," Becca said.

"What? But you said. . ."

Becca quickly darted in the bathroom where she hid for the entire lunch period.

Jake waited for about five minutes. . .five of the longest minutes of his life. Eventually the word reached Jake.

"She's not coming."

The event is a painful memory for him to talk about.

But it wasn't bullying.

People love to throw around the word *bullying*. Fact is, a lot of young people today are rude, mean, selfish. . .but not bullies.

I went to a workshop on bullying prevention from a professor at California State University, Sacramento where the presenter said something creative:

> If someone does something "unintentionally" hurtful, that's rude.
>
> If someone does something "intentionally" hurtful, and they do it once, that's mean!
>
> But when someone does something "intentionally" hurtful, you tell them to stop or you don't like it, and they keep doing it, that's bullying.

> ANY UNWANTED AGGRESSIVE BEHAVIOR(S) BY ANOTHER YOUTH OR GROUP OF YOUTHS WHO ARE NOT SIBLINGS OR CURRENT DATING PARTNERS THAT INVOLVES AN OBSERVED OR PERCEIVED POWER IMBALANCE AND IS REPEATED MULTIPLE TIMES OR IS HIGHLY LIKELY TO BE REPEATED.

Jake experienced a very hurtful experience, and most of the

school actually thought Becca was "lame" for doing what she did, but Becca didn't actually intend to hurt Jake. She was just fickle and acted selfishly, not considering how her actions affected others. In fact, afterward she felt terrible.

Becca's rejection of Jake was "unintentional." It wasn't a power play (other than the fact that she exercised the right to change her mind), and it wasn't ever repeated.

Bullying is all about power plays. And the more I interviewed bullies, the more I saw this firsthand.

POWER

Nick perfectly fit the axiomatic stereotype of "bully" in anyone's mind.

Nick was big.

He was an athlete.

He was popular.

He was a toolbag!

For Nick it began the summer before high school. He hit puberty, grew several shoe sizes, began lifting weights, and could grow a beard overnight.

Nick looked old for his age. He used to buy alcohol and cigarettes at fifteen. His size helped him get bumped to varsity in every sport as a freshman, which didn't hurt his popularity by any means. This gave him confidence. . .maybe overconfidence. In fact, Nick was voted "most outspoken" by his peers all four years of high school.

On the outside, Nick was living the dream; anybody would have wanted to be him.

On the inside, Nick felt like his life was falling apart.

Nick left his home at sixteen. His use of alcohol and drugs escalated to trying more illicit drugs. Nick dealt with his own pain by inflicting pain on others, but not just physically. Nick loved to "tease."

Nick told himself it was just teasing, but he knew his relentless mocking was hurting his victims. He told me, "I didn't care who you were, how big or small you were! Anything to get a laugh, belittle, or get attention."

Before long Nick was acting like the proverbial bully you've seen in every teen movie, repeatedly insulting others, knocking books or lunch trays out of people's hands, and instigating embarrassing pranks.

He quickly began meeting all the bullying criteria:

Aggressive behavior   ✓
Power play   ✓
Repeated   ✓

Nick had lots of moments he wasn't proud of, but the one he seemed most ashamed of was when he turned on his best friend.

Nick and Josh had been friends since they were kids. They lived next door to each other and hung out almost every day. The two shared their deepest, darkest secrets. . .until Nick became popular. As Nick changed, their relationship fell apart.

One day Nick was looking through pictures on his phone and found a video he took of Josh the year prior. In Nick's words, "Josh had this mad crush on this girl, but never had the nerve to tell her." Josh and Nick brainstormed ways he could ask her out, and Josh even practiced asking her out by asking out his sister's doll. Nick filmed this vulnerable moment.

When Nick found the video, he couldn't resist the opportunity. So he posted the video for all to see, and Josh was mortally embarrassed.

The episode was of course detrimental to Josh. He was now labeled "doll dater" by everyone, including Nick. Thanks to Nick, many *bystanders* were now becoming *bullies*. They would tease Josh repeatedly, hoping to feel better about their own status by dropping his status a few notches.

Aggressive behavior   ✓
Power play   ✓
Repeated   ✓

That's how it works. And Nick's story is far from unique.
Consider Chrissy.
Chrissy used to get picked on by the other girls at her school. When she asked her dad what she should do, he told her, "If they do

something mean to you, do something mean back to them. Stand up for yourself." And so she learned how to fight.

"This is when I became the bully," Chrissy told me. "For me the words 'stand up for yourself' meant to show you were the tough one. I was never the prettiest or the smartest, and never had the best clothes, but I could fight."

Chrissy became a scrapper, and she was pretty good at it.

She remembers one fight in particular when a girl was teasing Chrissy about her clothes. She marched straight up to her, punched her in the face, then jumped on top of her and kept punching.

"From that day on, if anyone made me upset, I just beat them up."

Chrissy's lack of conflict-management skills moved her from bullied to bully. Now she didn't just defend herself; she aggressively asserted her power by picking on others or intimidating them. Her defense mechanism had become her identity.

I was particularly sympathetic to Chrissy's story since she was initially being picked on. I could even relate to her dad's advice of "stand up for yourself," although I would have worded it a little differently.

But how is a parent to know when their child becomes a bully?

I'm sure Chrissy's dad never fathomed that Chrissy would start using fighting to solve problems.

Did he ever ask?

Did he ever follow up?

PARENTING A BULLY

In 2018 the TV channel A&E aired a show called *Undercover High* where seven "undercover adults" posed as high school students for a semester in Topeka, Kansas. The show unveiled some eye-opening realities for many parents, like exactly how much smartphones have changed teen culture in the last five years alone.

But these incognito adults embedded in the high school campus also discovered something else that surprised them and many researchers: *exactly how rampant bullying had become.*

In a candid interview, Erin, one of the undercover adults, shared her insight as someone who admittedly bullied others in the past:

I think for a lot of bullies it's not about looking to hurt someone in particular, but not being a target yourself, and just finding your niche. That's the shoes I filled. I wanted to stand out, and I wanted to be seen. I went to a large high school, so being someone who was under five feet, I knew that I needed to make myself seem big.[1]

Erin, like Chrissy, just wanted to survive. She didn't want to become *the bullied*. . .so for her, *bully* was a better option.

This is where the interview became especially intriguing. Erin was asked, "What would you suggest to parents if they think their teen is a bully?"

Erin's answer was something you're going to read repeatedly throughout this book: *engage your kids in dialogue about what's really happening in their lives.* Erin suggested parents actually ask who they're talking with, how they're treating others. Maybe even specifically, "What did you do in the hallway today?"

Erin said, "Parents always ask, 'How was school?' but don't think to dig deeper to what else is going on."[2]

Erin's insight is spot-on. In fact, all of the counselors I've interviewed and every single one of the studies I've read have two common denominators in their advice to parents: *notice and listen.*

We discussed how to "use our eyes and ears before our mouths" in the previous chapter. What specifically does this look like if our kid might possibly be a bully?

THE SIGNS WERE THERE

Earlier in the chapter I made the following claim:

In most situations the evidence of bullying was obvious to anyone who cared enough to notice and knew what to look for.

Let that sink in for a moment.

This book is full of stories and interviews where bullying went unnoticed. Sadly, whenever tragedy strikes—a suicide, a retaliation of violence—everyone looks back and concludes, "The signs were all there."

What signs?

I will repeat my contention: *In most situations the evidence of bullying was obvious to anyone who cared enough to notice and knew what to look for.*

Cared enough to notice:

I'm going to make a leap and assume you care enough to notice. Why? You have this book in your hands right now. And if you really care, then today when you come into contact with that kid you care so much about, I'll assume you'll practice noticing, "using your eyes and ears before your mouth," taking note of their attitude and behaviors, listening to what they talk about, and observing where they focus their attention. For many adults this will mean sliding aside our own devices for a given time during the day to take notice of our kids' world.

Knew what to look for:

What does today's bully look like? Is it always some big jock who pushes smaller kids around and steals their lunch money?

Girls typically engage in social power plays like belittling, ostracizing, and harassing. This might start with repeated name-calling, then graduate to shunning their victims from social circles—"You can't sit here." Sometimes this is just normal "drama." But when it becomes repeated, aggressive power plays (think of our three checkboxes), it's bullying.

Guys tend to be a little more physical, giving that hard bump with a stiff shoulder as they pass a weaker person in the hallway, slapping the back of the neck or legs, or even pushing and hitting. Not just one fight, but repeated, aggressive power plays (check, check. . .check).

Of course both guys and girls will dabble in both emotional and physical power plays, but typically it's a little more physical with guys and a tad more "drama" with girls.

Sometimes the levels a kid will sink to are jaw-dropping. Like "allergy bullying." Kids smear an unnoticeable trace of peanut butter across the keys of the keyboard of a kid with a peanut allergy. Or like the three fourteen-year-old Pennsylvania teens who in 2018 decided to target one of their classmates who had a severe pineapple allergy. One of these resentful girls rubbed pineapple all over her hands and deliberately high-fived the girl with the allergy.[3] The girl had to get a shot with an epinephrine pen and was taken to the hospital in an ambulance. The leader was charged with aggravated assault and three other felony charges. Her two friends are facing similar charges.[4]

Parents and teachers need to take notice of how each of their kids treat others, even when they don't think they're being watched. I'll reiterate: most kids aren't half as sly as they think they are. Adults can feign looking down at their own device while subtly keeping their eyes on their kids. Again, most adults don't pay much attention to young people, so young people aren't used to someone actually taking notice.

———————

Even if you don't see any obvious power plays, bullies will show early signs of bullying behaviors.

EARLY SIGNS YOUR KID MIGHT BE A BULLY
• LOW SELF-ESTEEM
• SELF-CENTEREDNESS—A LACK OF EMPATHY FOR OTHERS
• ANGRY OUTBURSTS—BECOMING FRUSTRATED WITH THEIR OWN PERSONAL PROBLEMS AND TAKING IT OUT ON OTHERS
• ATTENTION SEEKING—SPECIFICALLY SEEKING STATUS OR SUPERIORITY
• POWER PLAYS—WANTING CONTROL OVER OTHERS, SOMETIMES IN RETALIATION FOR BEING BULLIED BY SOMEONE ELSE
• HAVING A MOM OR DAD WHO PARENTS AT EITHER EXTREME—THE PARENT IS EITHER A BULLY OR A WEAKLING MANIPULATED AND CONTROLLED BY THE KID

Bullies usually show several of these signs. Having one of these characteristics doesn't make them a bully. In other words, if a kid just shows attention-seeking behaviors, that doesn't mean they're a bully. But if you see a kid with low self-esteem who hogs attention by repeatedly belittling others to make herself feel superior. . .then you might be seeing the early signs of a bully.

If you notice some of these signs, the next step is to engage the child in dialogue to gain a more accurate perspective on what you've observed. This requires less talking and more listening. Caring adults can have a much greater impact on kids when they move from a position of lecturing to a posture of listening. So when I say "engage your kids in dialogue," I'm emphasizing the word *dialogue*, which means two people interacting, not one person lecturing (which is a *monologue*).

We talked about what this looks like in the previous chapter: empathizing with young people, making them feel noticed and heard. This opens the door to dialogue with them about their world, revealing many of their thoughts and attitudes about others. It also might open up opportunities to discuss how their words can affect others.

The best way to open up these doors of dialogue is through questions.

"Tell me a little about your disagreement with Taylor yesterday."

"How did that make you feel?"

"How do you wish he would have treated you?"

"How did you respond?"

"If you had a do-over, would you respond the same way?"

Be careful not to switch to interrogation mode. These questions should be asked after you've already expressed empathy; you don't want to immediately switch back to blame.

But sometimes parents, teachers, and school administrators need to get to the bottom of a situation. This requires a bit of digging—and this is why it's so important for caring adults to notice and listen. A little investment of each can usually reveal any bullying behaviors at play. Once these are uncovered, it's time for the bully (or bullies) to be counseled.

~~CONFRONTING~~ COUNSELING A BULLY

Sometimes we need to remind ourselves that bullies need help just as much as the bullied. Trust me, acknowledging this truth can be difficult for me, especially when I see a mean kid abusing his power over someone weaker. This scenario brings up all kinds of hurt and makes me lose perspective.

As a quick aside, I'm going to mention this is where I really need to tap into God's power and give Him control over my reactions to others. The more I soak in His love, the more it overflows to others.

It also helps to know that many bullies are victims too, or at least humans with real struggles and insecurities of their own. Bullying takes an emotional toll on all involved. . .not just the bullied. In fact, a new study on the impact of cyberbullying on children and young people across thirty countries revealed that "cyberbullies—those that perpetrate such abuse—are around 20 percent more likely to have suicidal thoughts and to attempt suicide than non-perpetrators."[5]

It makes sense. Bullies not only are struggling with their own issues but are then plagued with guilt over how they're treating others.

Some bullies are getting bullied at home. Dad or Mom is laying into Junior. This makes Junior feel powerless, so he turns around and picks on the "easy to pick on" at school, who in turn goes home and kicks the dog. You might have heard the expression, "It rolls downhill" (I paraphrased just a bit).

For those of us who might struggle to empathize with a bully, consider that they might also be "the bullied," just like you or your child. They're just paying it forward.

No doubt you've heard the saying, "Hurt people *hurt people*." Consequently, bullies need our counsel.

The biggest help we can offer bullies is to teach them empathy. If we've already shown them empathy, they have an example to follow. But we can also coach them on what it looks like to step into someone else's shoes and consider others' needs before our own.

My friend Daniel Huerta, vice president of parenting and youth at Focus on the Family, has a great approach to bullies. Daniel is a licensed clinical social worker and counsels young people in his own practice. Whenever Daniel establishes a relationship with a bully and earns the right to counsel, he always uses "the fart analogy."

BREAKING WIND

Daniel says he likes to use this approach with kids who are not getting the concept. He simply asks, "How do you think people feel when you enter the room?"

Questions like this gauge how in tune kids are with their own behaviors.

If they don't seem to see how their own behaviors affect others, he asks, "How do you like it when someone walks into the room you're in and lets out a big ol' fart?"

This question usually draws a chuckle and creates some dialogue. No one likes smelling someone else's bodily functions, so the analogy works.

Daniel continues, "Whenever someone farts, they might feel better, but everyone else has to suffer. The same is true when we insult or belittle others. We might feel better, but they don't. They all want to leave the room."

Most bullies aren't getting the admiration and attention they're looking for, so they rely on destructive behaviors to gain control, attention, power, or affirmation.

Daniel has had to tell some of his clients, "Whenever you walk into a room, stop letting out farts. It might make you feel better, but no one else likes it. Bring pizza into a room, not your farts."

Don't be afraid to use this analogy with a bully you're counseling. After they exhibit some negative behaviors, you can pull them aside. "You just farted. Maybe you're feeling better, but we're not."

Sometimes bullies don't even grasp exactly what they have become. A caring adult or friend has to tell them. In their own minds they don't see themselves as "bullies." They might recognize that they're mean, but they justify it as a tactic to gain power or control. Sometimes they don't realize it because they have a group of followers who laugh, encouraging the behavior; but in reality these friends are afraid of the bully. So the bully contin-

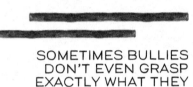

SOMETIMES BULLIES DON'T EVEN GRASP EXACTLY WHAT THEY HAVE BECOME.

ues the hurtful behaviors. They get some of the attention and power they're seeking but don't necessarily realize it's at the expense of the other person.

So many factors can create a bully. There are athletic bullies, rebellious bullies, wealthy bullies, low-income bullies, bullies with weak parents, bullies with bully parents. . .a combination of multiple factors. Bullies are complex. That's why sometimes bullies will need professional counseling.

When I was researching for this book, I found an article about a young girl named Rebecca who was bullied so severely she had to switch schools. Sadly, thanks to the world of social media, the tormentors followed her.

Rebecca finally committed suicide.

Several bullies were brought into custody, including a fourteen-year-old female who authorities said "lacked remorse." After Rebecca's death, the fourteen-year-old bully posted on Facebook: "Yes, I bullied Rebecca and she killed herself, but I don't give a f***."[6]

If you don't see any change in the bully's attitudes and behaviors, don't hesitate to contact a counselor for advice.

START EARLY

I encourage parents to begin having conversations with their kids about how to treat others early in life, like early elementary school. When they are in kindergarten and first grade, ask them about recess, who they played with, who they didn't play with, and how that made them feel. Don't turn every one of these conversations into a lecture; instead always lead them to discover their own answers, asking, "How did that make you feel?" and "How do you think they felt?" Help them get used to considering others' feelings (something we'll talk about in detail in the next chapter).

And don't beat yourself up if your kids are already in their teens. It's not too late to start engaging them in conversations about kindness (we'll explore what this looks like in the next chapter).

Realize that bullying is very often a learned behavior. One or both of their parents might be struggling with the same issues. Mom or Dad might become bullies at work, at school, or at PTA meetings. All the while, little Christina or little Jake is sitting there taking it all in.

Our actions will speak *waaaay* louder than our words. The more we model empathy, the more they will see how it looks day to day.

Hopefully our kids aren't bullies or bullied. But that makes them *bystanders*—and modeling empathy is just as important with *bystanders* to prevent them from developing into bullies.

Let's take a closer look at the bystander.

DISCUSSION QUESTIONS

1. What was one thing in this chapter that really stood out to you?

2. Bully, bullied, or bystander—which one were you? Which one is your kid?

3. Describe the differences you observe between rudeness, meanness, and bullying.

4. What makes a bully a bully?

5. What signs, subtle or blatant, have you observed in bullies?

6. What signs from Jonathan's list might you have missed in the past?

7. How can adults do a better job of teaching empathy?

8. What is one way you can model empathy this week?

CHAPTER 8
THE BYSTANDER
The chapter you might want to read with your kids

We will have to repent in this generation not merely
for the hateful words and actions of the bad people
but for the appalling silence of the good people.
–Martin Luther King Jr.

"I feel guilty about it every day," he told the crowd, a little choked by his own words.

The church youth group was captivated by Blake's vulnerability.

Blake seemed like a normal high school kid: decent grades, a soccer player, and from a good home. But this particular young man was obviously plagued with guilt.

"I saw him being made fun of every day," he said, "and I did nothing to stop it."

Blake went on to share about how the two of them used to be really good friends. They went to the same school, hung out at recess, and went to each other's birthday parties.

But then came middle school. In middle school you're judged by who you hang out with, and Blake's friend was definitely on the nerdy side. Blake's new soccer friends noticed this and began making fun of him.

"Is *he* your friend?"

"Why are you hanging out with him?"

So Blake cut off his relationship with his friend.

The situation took a turn for the worse. By high school Blake's athletic friends began regularly hurling insults at his old friend during lunch or in gym class. Blake never chimed in. He just watched in silence.

Blake confessed that he could still picture the look on his friend's face. He was haunted by the image.

As I heard Blake's story I winced, because I knew the story well.

Blake's old friend was my son.

―――

Blake was never a bully. He was the dictionary definition of a bystander, someone who watches and does nothing. Most kids on today's campuses probably fall into this category.

But bystanders hurt others just the same. It's a sin of omission. They know they should probably do something, but they don't.

I don't mean to imply Blake was a monster. Sadly, Blake's story isn't unique. Every campus I've visited is full of bystanders. The world is full of people who "don't want to get involved." And to Blake's credit, he recognized it. . .although a little too late.

Every interview I conducted revolved around stories involving three groups of people: a bully, the bullied, and entire classrooms or hallways or playgrounds full of people who watched and did nothing to interfere.

Bystanders are commonplace.

Why are bystanders so hesitant to get involved?

THE STRUGGLE IS REAL

Bystanders have their own sets of issues. If they're like today's typical teenager, they probably spend too much time staring at screens; struggle with feelings of insecurity; feel overwhelmed by school and the pressure to succeed; and look to social media, music, and entertainment media for fulfillment. And what is it they're hearing from every entertainment media source?

Do what's right for you.

Embrace yourself and just be you.

Some of these messages are literally pounding them daily. Nielsen revealed that Americans listened to an average of 32.1 hours of music per week in 2017.[1] That's 4.59 hours of music per day, saturating our kids with messages of "let go," "lose control," and "I can't stop." And that's just music; that doesn't include

Netflix, YouTube, social media, and other screen time.

What does all this add up to?

We're raising a generation of young people with low self-esteem who are being conditioned to selfishly live for the moment.

Drop them into a social situation where someone else is being mocked or targeted. Typical responses from bystanders include:

- "Whew! At least it's not me!"
- "That person being teased is actually pretty awkward."
- "I don't want to interfere because then I might be targeted as well."
- "The jokes being made are pretty funny."

Even if bystanders feel the conviction to say something or step in and defend the victim, those feelings are usually squashed because they require great risk.

How much risk?

Consider the fear of public speaking; now multiply it by ten. Not only does speaking up take guts, it risks long-term social consequences. The key phrase there is "long-term." Sticking up for a bullying victim isn't a one-shot deal.

Kids think about this—if you invite a kid to lunch "once," what happens if they want to eat with you again the next day? Are you committing to eat with that person for the rest of the year? What would that do to your own social standing? Would your friends even want to eat with you anymore?

They also wonder—if you defend a kid who is being teased for wearing Shaqs, the affordable shoes at Walmart, and you wear Le-Brons, which are well into the three-digit cost, are you being a hypocrite? Are you going to start wearing Shaqs to be more authentic? Are you supposed to change your entire wardrobe? There's nothing wrong with nice shoes. . .right?

I talked with a cheerleader about this issue, a kind, thoughtful girl who had a history of caring for people in need. I asked her if she ever felt torn if her popular crowd began teasing someone else. Her answer was intriguing.

"To be honest," she said, "it's not like I'm ever wanting to side with a bully; it's more that I don't necessarily want to start hanging out with someone who might be awkward and honestly difficult to get along with."

"TO BE HONEST," SHE SAID, "IT'S NOT LIKE I'M EVER WANTING TO SIDE WITH A BULLY; IT'S MORE THAT I DON'T NECESSARILY WANT TO START HANGING OUT WITH SOMEONE WHO MIGHT BE AWKWARD AND HONESTLY DIFFICULT TO GET ALONG WITH."

Some might gasp at her frank response, but she verbalized what many realistically think. Sometimes bullied kids are bullied because they are socially awkward or different. This social awkwardness is only perpetuated by isolation. In other words, after time, awkward kids become even more antisocial and engage in repellent behaviors.

So what happens?

When a bystander decides to cross the invisible lines in the cafeteria and sit next to someone alone and isolated, the conversation isn't always easy. It takes work. It's. . .awkward. It doesn't happen like in a Christian movie; it feels more like a *Seinfeld* episode.

What is the result?

Most likely the bystander checks that single good deed off their list, quietly thinking, *I'll never do that again*, and returning to their normal group for the next lunch.

SELF-ABSORBED

Bystanders are far from perfect. Sure, they might not necessarily "bully," but they dabble in social power plays. They throw a quick insult, then attempt to "cancel it out" with the phrase that erases all wrongs: "Just kidding."

"Nice shirt. Did you get it from the Goodwill clearance rack? . . . Just kidding."

This kind of trash-talking isn't anything new. The book of Proverbs even chimes in about it: "Like a maniac shooting flaming arrows of death is the one who deceives their neighbor and says, 'I was only joking'" (Proverbs 26:18–19).

In sports it's almost part of the game. You mess with the other team. It's a natural part of baseball, for sure.

But is this what we should expect with third graders on the kickball field?

How about sixth graders on the softball field?

Is it okay to "school someone"? In my research, many of the parents of younger boys shared that it was common for their kids' friends to insult each other, followed by, "You got burned!"

Harmless?

What about subtle gossip? "Is it just me, or do you think Shalyn has gained a lot of weight?"

Is it bullying. . .or just gossip?

"OMG. . .why is she wearing *that*?"

"Where did she get those shoes?"

"Mean" may be inherent, because kids begin these social power plays at an early age. I remember in first grade being assigned to bring an apple to class for a project. I don't remember the assignment, but I'll never forget the comparison games I experienced that day.

I brought in a green apple, because that's what my parents had in our fruit bowl on the kitchen counter. For some reason I had the only green apple in my class that day. I'm not sure why kids living in Denver, Colorado, in 1976 all favored red apples, but I do know that I was an outcast standing alone with a green apple.

In hindsight the way I was treated is actually hilarious. I can still remember the sarcastic comments my friends made.

"Why do you have a green apple?"

"I have a red apple. Red is much better than green."

"Green apples aren't even good."

These idiots had obviously never made an apple pie. Red Delicious are the worst! But it didn't matter. I was a lonely green living in a world of red, and I was immediately an outcast.

Was this bullying?

No, this was just normal self-absorbed behavior from a bunch of bratty little pie-hating first graders.

By fourth grade the meanness had graduated to shoes. My parents shopped at Kmart, and most of my friends' parents didn't.

Funny, we weren't necessarily poor, but my mom definitely was a bargain hunter. And up to this point Kmart shoes hadn't been a big deal. . .until a kid wearing Nikes noticed I was wearing Traxx.

Are you old enough to remember Traxx?

Traxx were the "Shaqs" of yesteryear. I wore Traxx most of my childhood. But once the Nike kids noticed my Traxx, the social lines were drawn in the sand. Within days I was literally being shunned because I wore Traxx.

I now realize this was borderline bullying. Certain kids repeatedly and aggressively teased me about wearing Traxx. I didn't like it, and they didn't care. They were just glad to be wearing Nikes.

I went home and told my mom, "I need some new shoes."

My mom looked at my shoes, confused, and asked, "What's wrong with your shoes? They look fine to me."

Luckily, my mom listened to her fourth-grade son share how the other kids were making fun of him for his shoes. I say "luckily," because from my fourth-grade perspective I felt "noticed and heard" by her. I don't know precisely why, but she decided to buy me some Nikes. They were royal blue with a yellow swoosh.

Was this the best move for a mom? Some might be hesitant to give in to this pressure to "fit in." *What are we teaching our kids?*

I honestly don't know if there is one right answer in these situations, but I'll tell you this: it's vital that parents make their kids feel noticed and heard. My mom did that for me back in 1980. . .and I can still remember the color of the Nikes. I think my mom gets a badge of excellence for that one.

A young girl named Rebecca told me about a similar incident when she was in fourth grade lining up outside of class after recess. One of the popular girls, whose name Rebecca will never forget, would always begin pointing at Rebecca's shoes and whispering to her group of friends. Within minutes Rebecca would feel like the whole class was laughing and pointing.

"My mom was a single mom at that time," Rebecca recalled, "and could barely scrape two pennies together, so we shopped at Kmart. While my shoes were the same style as their shoes, they did not have the tiny little name-brand blue rectangle on the back of them like these girls'."

One ringleader.

A handful of followers.

A classroom of snickering bystanders.

The dilemma surrounding so many of today's issues is that it isn't just one bully making fun of one kid. Sometimes bullying occurs by a whole crowd of jesters who join in to fit in. Sometimes bystanders inadvertently evolve into bullies. In fact, sometimes even teachers join in.

My youth worker friend Wayne has seen quite a bit of bullying throughout his years of ministry. Wayne was bullied a lot as a kid, and he knows what it looks like. He also recognizes that parents and teachers can make a huge impact either way.

When Wayne was in high school, he had a particular math teacher who made the situation far worse. She was overly tolerant of banter in the classroom. When kids made fun of him, she didn't intervene. So kids became bolder and hurled cruel insults at him for everyone to hear. Sometimes the teacher even laughed at the jokes.

Wayne felt betrayed and alone.

Some teachers might think, *This is all in good fun.*

Is it? Are you sure?

When does teasing cross the line?

Go back to the characteristics of bullying:

Aggressive behavior	✓
Power play	✓
Repeated	✓

Take notice. Is the teasing harmless jests from friends? Do you ever see these kids hanging out together and having fun? Don't be confused if you see the victim laughing. He or she might just be trying to save face. If one kid is being insulted *repeatedly*, it might not be in good fun. Don't allow those doors to even open.

Bottom line: Restrict *repetitive* teasing. One wisecrack doesn't make someone a bully. But if you see repetitive teasing, you need to intervene.

Yet adult intervention doesn't eliminate bullying, simply because adults can't be there 24-7. That's why the best resource we have is our

WE NEED TO EQUIP BYSTANDERS TO ADVOCATE FOR KIDS WHO ARE BULLIED.

kids. We need to equip bystanders to advocate for kids who are bullied.

I firmly believe today's young people are the cure for bullying. I speak to young people at countless events encouraging and equipping them to stop bullying at the outbreak.

Bystanders don't need to do what their name implies: *stand by.* They can *stand up* and do something.

Let's look at what that actually looks like.

PEER INTERVENTION

When bystanders stand up and do something, it's called peer intervention. I use the term *peer intervention* because those two words have become buzzwords in bullying research as researchers have come to realize how much difference one kid can make.

We can help our kids truly make a bullying breakthrough by teaching them the 5 Rs:

1. Recognize the effects of bullying

I recently finished writing a novel about a school shooting titled *Bystander.* The book follows three adults and three students the week of a school shooting on a high school campus. The perspective switches from a bully, to bystanders, and finally to a bullied kid pushed beyond the tipping point.

I wrote the book for one reason: to cultivate empathy. I want parents and young people to step into the shoes of others.

Much recent research has revealed that increased screen time is slowly killing empathy. The more people stare at screens and communicate using screens, the more socially hindered they become. We need to help young people look up from their screens, notice others, and think beyond their own little world.

Whenever I speak to young people about bullying, I always tell plenty of stories. Stories help us all look beyond our own perspective and see through the eyes of others. Stories cultivate compassion and empathy.

Parents and teachers can raise awareness by talking about the effects of bullying and sharing stories that help young people consider the perspective of others. Many bystanders have never paused to think through the ramifications of laughing at someone, teasing them. . .or watching and doing nothing.

Help your kids see the reality of what bullying does to the one being bullied. Share stories that help them look through the eyes of others, then ask questions like, "Do you know anyone who gets bullied?"

2. Realize *you* can make a huge impact.

One kid can make a huge difference.

Really.

Just one.

Countless studies show that one friend is enough to prevent the downward slide toward depression.

A report in the journal *Development and Psychopathology* revealed, "Just one friend is enough to buffer an anxious, withdrawn child against depression. And it doesn't have to be a particularly close friend—not an intimate or a confidant, as an adult would understand it, just some kind of social connection with someone their own age."[2]

Just one friend made the difference. Kids who had no friends were by far at the highest risk for depression and anxiety, according to the two-year study. And the biggest asset against depression was friendship.

We need to help our kids understand just how powerful their simple acts of friendship can be.

Another study funded by the National Institute of Justice showed that peers can be the most effective at intervening when they see bullying take place. Peer intervention "may be the most effective counter to aggressive and micro-aggresive behavior."[3]

Maybe a peer steps in and says, "Hey, that's not okay." Or if that's too risky, maybe they approach the victim later and say, "Would you like to talk?" Those simple gestures are by far the most effective in helping those experiencing bullying.

Funny. Neither of these studies show adults as the most effective cure for bullying.

A friend is the most effective.

Just *one* friend makes a difference.

So where do these simple acts of friendship begin?

3. Resolve not to bully others.

Most movements begin with a decision, a commitment, a "resolve." I think of Daniel in the Bible when he was plucked from the safety of his home and plopped down into a world brimming with temptations. He made a decision, a commitment. He "resolved not to defile himself" (Daniel 1:8).

Whenever I speak to today's young people, I give them the opportunity to make a public commitment. It's one thing to be moved with compassion. Commitment puts feet to those feelings.

Compassion without action is nothing.

I'm reminded of the powerful scene in the movie *Hotel Rwanda*—the true-life story of a Rwandan hotel manager who housed more than one thousand Tutsi refugees, protecting them from the Hutu militia.

The movie includes a sobering scene between the hotel manager, Paul (Don Cheadle), and a news photographer, Jack (Joaquin Phoenix), who has just filmed the ugly reality of the atrocities happening in Rwanda:

> **Paul Rusesabagina:** I am glad that you have shot this footage and that the world will see it. It is the only way we have a chance that people might intervene.

Jack: Yeah and if no one intervenes, is it still a good thing to show?

Paul Rusesabagina: How can they not intervene when they witness such atrocities?

Jack: I think if people see this footage they'll say, "Oh my God, that's horrible," and then go on eating their dinners.[4]

It happens all the time. People might be moved with compassion. . .but not moved off their butts to do anything about it.

Resolve is the decision to take action. Which brings us to specific actions kids can take. . .

4. Refuse to join in.

One of the most important actions kids can engage in is *not engaging*.

Bystanders have the ability and responsibility to avoid any behaviors that build up bullies by tearing down others. Bullies thrive on attention and affirmation. Give them neither.

So help bystanders learn to avoid the following:

- laughing at jokes at the expense of others
- listening to rumors, gossip, or hate speech from anyone
- physically standing with a group that is mocking or gossiping about others

Refusing to join doesn't always necessitate speaking up and saying, "Hey, this isn't okay." Sometimes bystanders can walk away, or in class they can just keep their attention on their schoolwork.

If bullies don't receive any affirmation or attention for their mean behavior, they'll usually stop said behavior.

5. Reach out to someone who is hurting or alone.

The best bullying advice I have ever heard comes from Paul's letter to the Philippians in the Bible:

> *Do nothing out of selfish ambition or vain conceit. Rather, in humility value others above yourselves, not looking to your own interests but each of you to the interests of the others. In your relationships with one another, have the same mindset as Christ Jesus.*
> (Philippians 2:3–5)

Can you imagine if everyone actually lived out this advice? We could cut down on a whole lotta bullying for sure!

It's amazing what simple acts of kindness can do. But these acts are rare. Kids are all about "mine!" Put out two pieces of cake for your two kids and both will grab for the bigger piece. It's uncommon to find a kid who genuinely offers the bigger piece to their brother or sister.

At school it's the same. Kids typically value self above others, not the inverse.

But this generation of young people really wants to do something and make a difference. Often, they just don't know how. It's an interesting tension. They're self-centered but want to help others. Sometimes a caring adult can help connect the dots showing how to get from A to B.

What would it look like to invite that awkward kid over to hang out after school. . .knowing full well that it might be awkward?

Passages like the one from Philippians 2 are impactful as we teach our kids how to reach out. *Be humble. Consider others better than you. This is what Jesus modeled.*

Showing humility and *valuing others above self* are concepts kids don't spend much time thinking about, but you'll be surprised how much kids will rise up when given the opportunity to demonstrate these values.

During spring break the middle school kids at my church serve the homeless in needy areas of San Francisco by doing something you don't see very often—they wash their feet. Imagine seeing a junior high boy sitting on the ground washing the feet of a homeless man and then giving him new socks. I think that's probably the dictionary definition of *humility*. For these kids it's just doing what Jesus modeled in John 13.

It's interesting how these kids make that connection of what humility looks like in other venues like school or even in their homes. Once you wash a homeless person's feet, standing up and doing something for the bullied is much easier.

THE DECISION

Can one kid really make a difference?

It's more than just research and articles—it's happening all over the country. Parents and teachers shared with me numerous examples of kids who made a decision to do something about bullying, either as individuals or as part of a school program (and I'll be sharing some fun examples of these "peer counseling" programs in my final chapter). Bystanders have amazing potential to stand up and make an impact in the lives of hurting kids. Bystanders don't just have to "stand by." One friend really does make a difference.

When I was in high school, that "one friend" was Matt. Matt wasn't the most popular kid on campus, but he decided he was going to care for others no matter what anybody said.

I'll never forget looking across campus one day and seeing Matt rolling a kid in a wheelchair to his class. Other kids were looking at Matt like, *What are you doing that for, extra credit?* But Matt didn't care. When he saw someone in need, Matt acted.

Matt was in weights class with many of the football players, bench pressing and squatting enormous poundage and getting high-fives of congratulations. But at lunchtime, Matt would sit with a group of outcasts. Matt broke the unspoken lines of separation. He didn't show prejudice in any way.

One kid made a decision to treat everyone the same.

Did Matt rid an entire campus of bullies?

No. Bullying still happened.

But Matt made a world of difference to the handful of lives he touched every day. I'll never forget that.

Can you imagine what that campus would have looked like with even two "Matts"?

Three?

Matt was a *bystander* who provided real help to *the bullied*.

Let's take a closer look at this group of kids who are targeted, mocked, and laughed at.

DISCUSSION QUESTIONS

1. What was one thing in this chapter that really stood out to you?

2. Why are bystanders so hesitant to get involved?

3. When does a "snickering bystander" become a bully?

4. Is it ever okay for a parent or teacher to participate in teasing a kid in good fun? Explain.

5. How can reading an article about bullying or reading a book about a school shooting help increase empathy?

6. What are some ways we can give bystanders an opportunity to "make a difference"? (Note: The last chapter of this book provides several examples.)

7. What is one thing you can do to encourage a bystander this week?

8. Who is one kid who might need to read this chapter with you? (I've included an extra set of discussion questions on the following page.)

KIDS' DISCUSSION QUESTIONS
Questions to dialogue about with your kids

1. What was one thing in this chapter that really stood out to you?

2. Why is it that so many bystanders simply "stand by" instead of "standing up" for someone who is bullied?

3. Describe a time you saw someone being teased repeatedly or bullied.

4. When does gossiping or laughing about someone else become bullying?

5. Why do you think just one friend can make a difference in the life of someone who is picked on constantly?

6. Who is someone you know who might really need a friend?

7. What would be the difficult part of befriending this person?

8. What would it look like to invite an awkward kid over to hang out after school, knowing full well that your time together might be awkward?

9. What is something you can do this week to "stand up" instead of just "standing by"?

CHAPTER 9
THE BULLIED
Spotting the warning signs

You may choose to look the other way,
but you can never say again that you did not know.
–William Wilberforce

Zach was more active than both his brothers and always played sports, but for some reason he gained weight much quicker. Doctors eventually diagnosed him with a medical condition—his body stored more fat than normal. Zach had to work twice as hard as most kids to keep his weight under control.

But that meant most of his childhood Zach dealt with an onslaught of fat jokes.

Zach, now twenty, opened up to me about his childhood.

"I lived with a lot of 'Cheeseburger Boy' jokes through elementary school," he shared. "And that was probably one of the nicer names. The worst were in middle school and high school when they made fun of my chest. They said I had 'tits.' My friends called me 'Brother Jugs.' It seemed playful, but when everyone is saying it. . ."

Zach struggled to articulate his feelings.

I gave him a moment.

"Later in high school it wasn't as intense," he said, regaining his composure, "but in elementary and middle school it tore me apart."

"So what did you do?" I asked.

"I couldn't do anything. If I told on them, I was a wuss for tattling. When I did tell the noon duty aids, they told me, 'Oh, just ignore them. They don't mean it.' When I told my mom, she would just ask, 'Did you tell anyone at school?' I'd say, 'Yes. They told me to ignore it.' And she'd say, 'Well, that's good advice.'"

Zach was experiencing what countless bullying victims face.

No one truly understood.

No one was really listening.

"Did anything help?" I asked.

"In middle school a kid named Ryan was trying to throw a football at my stomach in gym class. I was pretty good at sports, so I actually caught his throw. He said, 'Nice catch, fat a**!' So I walked up to him, punched him in the face, jumped on top of him, and kept swingin'. I never had a problem with him after that."

"Did that help?" I asked.

Zach pondered the question.

"Well, I never dated, never went to dances, never went to prom. I know that's all 100 percent from being overweight," he said. "It doesn't matter how much I succeeded in sports. It's just hard to believe in yourself when you're being torn down every day."

How can we help the countless "Zachs" in this world?

Is sports the answer?

What about fighting back?

How could the noon duty aids and Zach's parents have helped?

How did they miss the warning signs that Zach was being pushed beyond the tipping point?

Let's dive a little deeper into the world of the bullied; then let's look at some common warning signs that your child might be the victim of bullying.

BOYS WILL BE BOYS

Adam loved Disney films, especially *Monsters, Inc.* That's why for Halloween he wanted to be Mike Wazowski.

Adam was in fourth grade.

The costume was hilarious: a big, round green guy with one big eye. Adam couldn't wait to wear it to his school Halloween party.

He saved his money for weeks and finally bought the costume. When he got it home he immediately tried it on and began dancing around the room, making his little sisters laugh.

What fourth grader wouldn't love this?

Apparently a lot of them.

When Adam showed up at the school Halloween party, most of his classmates weren't dressed up as Disney characters. The party was for fourth through sixth graders. There were ten- and twelve-year-olds dressed like twenty-year-olds: pirates, sexy nurses, football players, cheerleaders, gangsters. . .and maybe go-go-dancers? (Not sure, actually. What costume is a sixth-grade girl in a short skirt, fishnet stockings, and a feathered hat?)

But they were all glaring at Adam.

"Look at the big green dork!"

"Ha! Nice costume, you fat-tard!"

"Are you serious?"

Kids laughed and pointed.

Adam's confidence quickly faded. He tried to avoid the mocking, but literally everywhere he went his classmates jeered.

Finally Adam tugged on his dad's shirt.

"Can we go?"

Apparently fourth-grade boys can't be silly or cute. Boys have to be cool and confident.

Adam didn't know much about being cool or confident. He had spent most his childhood playing with imaginary friends and having tea parties with two younger sisters.

Adam didn't fit the cool stereotype.

Imaginative and creative boys have it rough. If you aren't good at throwing a pigskin or shooting an orange ball through a hoop. . .what good are you?

I remember watching my son play with his friends in elementary school. Most of the other boys were playing soccer or dodgeball. Alec was playing velociraptor!

There was my son, a happy, imaginative kid prancing around the playground leaning over, swaying his velociraptor head back and forth with his arms retracted to his chest like the creature he was imitating.

Some kids laughed at him, shaking their heads.

Alec was too busy chasing brontosauruses to notice.

Where are creative kids supposed to play today?

One of the elementary boys in my neighborhood is often playing outside with his brother and sister. Actually, the word *with* is probably incorrect. His brother and sister are usually playing basketball or kicking a soccer ball around while he frolics in the front lawn pretending he's in some far-off land battling imaginary creatures.

I saw him last week at church after five days of rain.

"I didn't see you outside in the rain last week," I said. "What's your favorite thing to do when it's raining? Stay in and play video games?" (I inadvertently was stereotyping.)

I'll never forget his response.

His eyes lit up and he said, "Or use my imagination!"

My first thought was, *This kid is awesome!* Sadly, my immediate second thought was, *This kid is going to get teased by every one of his classmates.*

That's what happened to Ethan. Ethan was constantly teased by his fifth-grade classmates. They called him a "girl" and told him how much he "sucked" at any sport he tried.

It was a daily routine. A group of boys actually followed him around at recess and told him how much they hated him.

Ethan finally talked with his parents about the teasing, and they acted immediately. They brought the issues to the attention of the teacher and eventually the principal, who were both, unfortunately, very chummy with the other boys' parents. So all the principal did was assure Ethan's parents, "The boys are just playing. I promise you, these are great families."

And the issue was swept under the rug.

The bullying grew worse, culminating during recess one day when three of the boys actually grabbed Ethan, pulled his hood over his head, and called him a "retard."

Ethan snapped. He slapped one of the boys in the face, pushed the others away, and fled.

Wonder of wonders, now the principal had an issue. She called Ethan into a room *with* the three boys who were doing the bullying and asked the three boys to explain what had happened, and they claimed they were innocently playing on the playground when Ethan started pushing them and slapping them for no reason. Ethan tried to tell his side of the story, but the principal cut him off.

The principal sent an email to Ethan's mom outlining how Ethan would be reprimanded. Ethan's mom replied with questions.

No response.

And now Ethan was on the principal's hit list. Ethan couldn't blink without the principal jumping in.

I talked with Ethan's mom about the situation.

"Things became so bad between the bullies and the school principal that I was physically ill every time I dropped my kids off at school," she said. "My kids were both begging me to let them stay home from school. And there was crying every night at bedtime."

Ethan's family changed schools, and Ethan didn't have any problems at the new school.

Is changing schools the answer?

What if changing schools doesn't help?

"ON THE SPECTRUM"

Some kids get teased wherever they go, especially kids on the spectrum. "On the spectrum" is a term I heard frequently talking with parents about bullying issues. It refers to kids with autism spectrum disorders, ranging from autistic—the most severe of the disorders—to Asperger syndrome, sometimes called "high-functioning autism."

My sister-in-law, a speech pathologist, has told me that one of the hardest things to deal with when working with kids on the spectrum is their social skills. So many of these children have quirks and behaviors that make them stand out in a crowd, especially among their peers. Some might have an aversion to loud noises and choose to wear sound-dampening headphones. Others may be sensitive to certain textures and pull away from art projects or outdoor play on the grass. And some may have food sensitivities and not like to have certain foods touch other foods. All of these differences often result in their being teased because they act differently from their peers. Beyond sensory issues, kids on the spectrum also lack some of the intuitive social understanding that most children develop naturally. They may not understand sarcasm or nonverbal facial expressions, and may read a comment such as "Nice job, Brandon," at face value when it was actually meant as an insult.

While bullying at school is something most kids face at some point in their lives, kids on the spectrum encounter an entirely different level of bullying, both in severity and in duration. *Retard* seems to be the word of choice from bullies targeting kids on the spectrum. It's the word parents of kids on the spectrum seemed to recount the most.

"Nice one, retard!"

Kids on the spectrum often struggle socially, which makes them easy targets. Their social awkwardness can make it difficult for bystanders to befriend them, so they are commonly alone, which only makes the situation worse.

But in most cases a caring adult makes the difference. A parent, a grandparent, a teacher. Someone patient who loves the child unconditionally and walks through life with them.

I heard some great testimony from parents of kids on the spectrum who discovered activities their kids actually enjoyed, hobbies or even sports that connected them with other kids with similar interests.

Josh, a high school sophomore on the spectrum, found the ultimate Frisbee team to be something he thoroughly enjoyed. It was more laid back than typical high school sports, which fit his personality well.

Ultimate Frisbee was perfect for Josh his freshman year. It got him active and part of a team. His parents were thrilled. But his sophomore year he began to encounter some struggles, specifically with Caden, the captain, who found Josh difficult. One day at practice Caden and the others were bantering back and forth, predominantly healthy teasing. But then one of the kids accidently splattered some mud on Josh's new sweatshirt. Josh reacted poorly, making it a bigger deal than most kids would have, so Caden dipped a Frisbee in mud and threatened to throw it at Josh.

Josh said, "If you do, I'll quit."

Caden turned to the team and asked, "All in favor of me throwing this Frisbee at Josh so he quits the team?"

The team members all raised their hands.

Caden threw the Frisbee, and Josh kept his word. He quit right then and there.

It's amazing how often bystanders get sucked into bullying behaviors.

It's even more amazing how often adults will simply ignore the behavior, saying, "Boys will be boys."

But bullying isn't just a male activity.

MEAN GIRLS

Melanie and Jessica seemed inseparable. At least until Jessica got her driver's license the summer before her junior year. Then she began hanging out with Paige. . .and drinking, vaping, and smoking pot.

Soon Melanie barely heard from Jessica at all.

School started, and Melanie saw Jessica walking with her new friend Paige in the hallway.

"Hey, Jess. How was your summer?" Mel asked genuinely.

Paige mimicked Mel's voice. *"Hey, Jess. How was your summer?"*

Jessica laughed, but answered Melanie: "Boring."

Paige looked Melanie up and down. "D*mn girl, what the h*ll is wrong with your nose? It's like you're a toucan or something."

Jessica giggled for the second time at her friend's expense.

Mel was speechless. *This girl is toxic. What does Jess see in her?* But Mel was also truly hurt. Apparently Paige knew exactly where to poke a girl. Mel had always been severely self-conscious about her nose, and Jess knew it.

Did Jess tell her?

Mel just turned and walked away.

The next day as Mel walked down the hall, she heard a voice behind her squawk like a bird.

"Nice beak, Toucan!"

Mel whipped around to see Paige and Jess ducking behind a crowd of girls, laughing.

Later that week Jessica's car pulled up next to Mel as she walked home. Paige was in the passenger seat rolling down the window.

"Do you have any Froot Loops, Toucan?"

Mel tried to ignore it, but the girls followed her home, squawking and hurling insults.

When Mel got home, she burst into tears. She told herself she didn't care what Paige thought. *But why Jessica? She's my friend, isn't she?*

The harassment continued, and Mel finally told her mom.

Mel's mom went to the principal, but that only made the situation worse. The principal did what so many principals do. She called a meeting with all three girls, asking Jessica and Paige for their side of the story. The meeting ended with a warning to all three girls. "You guys just keep clear of each other and mind your own business. Melanie, you just go to your classes and go home, and Jessica and Paige, you do the same. This campus is plenty big for all of you, and we don't need any of this foolishness."

Then she ended with a question that had to be a joke.

"Everybody friends now?"

Jessica and Paige answered immediately. "Of course."

An hour later Jessica's car pulled up at Mel's bus stop and Paige got out, walked up to Mel, shoved her on the ground, and unloaded more obscenities than a Tarantino movie.

"So you ran to the principal?" Paige yelled. "Are you gonna tell her about this too, Toucan?"

All the kids at the bus stop laughed.

Mel gathered her stuff quietly and went home.

Mel told me, "I didn't tell my mom that time. I didn't tell anyone." Mel had learned that sharing her hurt would only make it worse.

Another teen ignored.

It's hard to grasp how these kinds of incidents are missed. Like the situation faced by Ally Del Monte, a sixteen-year-old who tried to commit suicide after being cyberbullied so severely she didn't see any other alternative.

The cruel jests began when she was eight years old. "I was really overweight," she told ABC News. "My friends thought it was funny and would exclude me from the playground. They would make fun of me."[1]

When Ally entered the online world, the bullying quickly followed.

"It's very public, it's very humiliating, and it's 24-7," psychotherapist Robi Ludwig said. "It's not like you can go home, close the door, and pretend it's not happening. . . . That's what makes it so damaging. . .for a young kid that can't really see that difficult times will pass."[2]

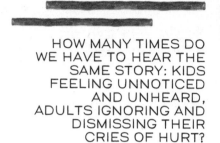

HOW MANY TIMES DO WE HAVE TO HEAR THE SAME STORY: KIDS FEELING UNNOTICED AND UNHEARD, ADULTS IGNORING AND DISMISSING THEIR CRIES OF HURT?

Ally received messages every week telling her she was worthless and that no one cared. "One night was really bad," Ally shared. "I had 172 messages on there telling me to kill myself. . . . And I said 'OK.' I tried to take a bunch of pills that night, and I almost died because of it."[3]

How many times do we have to hear the same story: kids feeling unnoticed and unheard, adults ignoring and dismissing their cries of hurt?

How can we be proactive about recognizing these cries?

It begins with just that—recognizing.

WARNING SIGNS

I kept hearing the same words over and over again in my interviews with victims of bullying.

"I didn't tell anyone."

And even if they did tell someone. . .

"My dad told me to ignore it."

Most victims of bullying don't explicitly tell their parents they are being bullied. They might allude to it or make subtle comments, but often parents miss it because it's not even on their radar.

In a world where bullying is common and its reach is extending to the devices in our kids' pockets, parents need to keep watch for warning signs and listen for implicit hints and clues that their child might be being bullied.

Let's review a few of the warning signs.

THE VERBALIZING OF INSECURITIES

Bullying is an aggressive attack on the victim's self-esteem. So even if kids aren't sharing about bullying, they often will display signs of insecurities they are feeling.

One mom told me how she noticed her daughter Emma sucking in her belly in front of the mirror while getting ready for bed. When Emma saw her mom standing there, she asked, "Mom, am I skinny enough?"

Emma was eight years old.

Emma's mom soon discovered Emma was being ruthlessly teased about her weight by a group of girls at school.

Emma wasn't fat by any means. She was not even slightly chubby. But a particular girl at school was obsessed with her own weight, announcing it at the lunch table every day, pulling out her own "diet food," and criticizing the other girls for what their moms had packed them for lunch. (It's pretty obvious when kids are displaying learned behavior from their own homes.)

Emma never shared this with her mom until her mom specifically asked. It only came out once she began talking about her weight and her mom finally asked, "Why are you worried so much about your weight, baby girl?"

We need to keep our eyes and ears open for kids verbalizing or displaying insecurities that might reflect what they're hearing from someone else.

CHANGE IN FRIEND GROUPS

Sometimes we'll notice our kids aren't hanging out with certain friends or friend groups anymore. This can be a sign that they are struggling socially or even being shunned by certain kids.

The mom of a little girl named Sophia noticed this when Sophia stopped talking about her friend Madison. Sophia didn't show any other signs of being bullied, but one day her mom just wondered, *How come I don't hear about Madison anymore?*

So she subtly mentioned to Sophia, "I don't hear you talk about Madison anymore."

Sophia's body language immediately shifted. Her head dropped, and she wouldn't look at her mom. "I don't really play with her anymore."

Sophia's mom calmly asked, "Why? Did something happen?"

Sophia didn't answer right away. She pondered the situation and finally shared, "She just wants to play with her other friends more."

Eventually Sophia's mom discovered that Madison would snatch Sophia's crayons during class, insult her, and then say mean things about her to other girls, trying to make Sophia feel like an outcast. As a result, Sophia began hanging out all by herself on the playground each day. Soon she didn't have any friends.

Sophia never verbalized any of this. Her mom only discovered it when she didn't hear about Madison anymore.

Obviously it's not a surefire sign of bullying every time our kids start hanging out with new friends. But usually there are reasons behind this kind of change. Sometimes it can be chalked up to normal "drama."

Other times, however, it can be caused by something unhealthier, as in the case of a self-assured fourth grader named Amanda. Amanda's mom thought there was no way Amanda could ever be pushed around by a bully, but then Amanda encountered a very vindictive mean girl named Olivia. The two started as friends, but every time Amanda played with someone else, Olivia went mental. Naturally her overreaction pushed Amanda away, so Olivia began lavishing Amanda with gifts, trying to buy back her friendship. One day Amanda received a gift from Olivia in the morning, and when Amanda played with another girl at recess, Olivia demanded the gift back and then promptly threw it in the trash to make a point.

Amanda's mom noticed Amanda didn't talk about Olivia anymore. It was only after asking her about it that she heard about some of Olivia's antics.

Sometimes a change in friend groups is a sign of repeated aggressive behaviors.

AVOIDANCE OF SCHOOL OR DECLINING GRADES

One of the telltale signs of bullying is when your child doesn't want to go to school anymore. Often they won't tell you why. You'll just begin hearing a lot of excuses.

"My stomach really hurts again."

"I've got a migraine."

"I don't like school anymore."

This is always a tough situation for parents because sometimes our kids might really be sick. They might even need medical attention. But if the doctor doesn't find any physical ailments, it's good to sit down and try to discover if something bigger is going on.

I've talked with parents whose kids were "A" students their whole lives, then all of a sudden their child was missing school and barely pulling off Cs. Very often this is a sign of something traumatic happening in a child's life. If it's not something at home, chances are it could be a relationship at school.

"TEASING"

Sometimes parents will observe teasing that crosses a line.

The word *teasing* can be misleading. It almost conveys that "it's all in good fun." But as we discussed earlier in this book, when teasing becomes an aggressive and/or repetitive power play, it morphs into bullying.

When I was in sixth grade, my dad came to one of my soccer practices to watch me play. I didn't even know he was there, but he was watching the way I interacted with my friends.

When practice was over, he told me, "Jonathan, I don't want you hanging out with Dean anymore."

I didn't even argue or ask for an explanation (and I almost always argued). I just said, "Okay."

My dad's demand was actually a relief. Dean was a textbook bully. All he did was tear everyone else down to build himself up. I don't know if my dad had objected to that or to the foul language and crude analogies Dean always chose—this kid would make a sailor cringe. But I had no problem hearing my dad confirm what

I was already feeling.

Sometimes mere "name-calling" is much more than that. Watch out for repetitive and aggressive power plays disguised as "teasing."

INCREASED ANXIETY AND/OR DEPRESSION

In a world where anxiety and depression have risen to unprecedented levels among young people, it might be hard to spot angst specifically from bullying.

Teen anxiety is off the charts. Back in 1985, the Higher Education Research Institute at UCLA began asking incoming college freshmen if they "felt overwhelmed by all I had to do" during the previous year. "In 1985, 18 percent said they did. By 2010, that number had increased to 29 percent. Last year [2016], it surged to 41 percent."[4]

Earlier in the book I presented research indicating that the growing use of social media and mobile devices is catalyzing this unprecedented increase in teen anxiety and depression. Some of this is the pressure young people are feeling to "measure up" to everyone else. But some of it stems from the mean comments and comparison games young people are engaging in.

One of the counselors I interviewed said, "I can always tell which kids are engrossed in social media. Young people's moods are forged by the amount of time they spend online."

A sobering observation.

If you notice your kids being more withdrawn, it's a good idea to discover why. If your son is spending large amounts of time alone and isolated in his room, it's likely for reasons that aren't good.

Anxiety and depression just might be a sign that your kid is having difficulty socially in one way or another.

SUBTLE CONFESSIONS

Sometime our kids will verbalize hints about bullying without actually telling us the whole story.

"Logan has been messing with me lately."

The key to getting the rest of the story is not overreacting. Instead, try to become an empathetic listener, not to fix, solve, or correct, but to uncover and to make your child feel noticed and heard. By creating a climate where they feel safe to share with you, you'll open the door to dialogue where you can hear the rest of the story.

CHANGE IN EATING HABITS

Changes in kids' eating habits can occur for several different reasons. One, kids can literally lose their appetite because of mental anguish.

But sometime parents will notice kids are hungry when they get home from school. This could be because they skipped lunch in fear of walking through certain areas, or because their lunch money was stolen or their lunch tray dumped again.

It's not uncommon for bullied kids to hang out in the library to avoid confrontations with others.

UNEXPLAINABLE INJURIES

It's pretty obvious your kid was fighting when he comes home with a black eye, but also watch for unexplained scratches or bruises.

Is your kid wearing long sleeves on a 90-degree day? This could also be a sign of self-harm.

LOST OR DESTROYED BOOKS, CLOTHING, PHONES, WATCHES, AND OTHER JEWELRY

Is the cover of your son's history book torn? Why?

Is your daughter beginning to lose things when she's always been responsible?

One of the telltale behaviors of bullies is knocking books out of others' hands. It's probably the most common element I heard in the interviews I conducted. So take notice if your kids' books or folders are dirty or ripped.

So what do we do when we notice any of these signs?

Let's look at some healthy responses. In fact, I'm going to devote an entire chapter to ways we can help the bullied.

DISCUSSION QUESTIONS

1. What was one thing in this chapter that really stood out to you?

2. Do you think a bunch of guys calling their friend "Brother Jugs" was harmless? Do you think they knew what it was doing to their friend? Explain.

3. How can schools take better care of kids who aren't athletic and are destined to be picked on in gym class?

4. How can we help prevent kids from bullying kids "on the spectrum"?

5. Which do you personally have a more difficult time dealing with, "bad boys" or "mean girls"? Why?

6. Which of the warning signs have you spotted in your kids? Is there one you didn't know about?

7. Are there any other signs you have noticed that Jonathan didn't list?

8. What is one thing you can do to proactively watch for these signs this week?

CHAPTER 10
REAL-WORLD SOLUTIONS
Ten tools to help bullied kids

We've jumped into the minds of *the bully, the bystander,* and *the bullied,* and I've given you heaps of practical tips to help diverse kids in various contexts. Now I'd like to focus specifically on the kids who are being bullied or targeted. Remember, bullying features the following characteristics:

Aggressive behavior ✓
Power play ✓
Repeated ✓

What are some real ways parents and teachers can help these hurting kids?

Let's look at ten.

1. DON'T FREAK OUT.

Overreaction never helps.

If you happen to notice your child showing some of these signs, suppress the urge to freak out!

"Why are you eating a snack? Did someone steal your lunch? I'm calling the police!"

Maybe your kid is just hungry. Do you have a teen boy? They can eat more than a full-grown great white shark.

Don't freak out. Your overreaction slams shut any doors you have opened.

Instead, convert your overreaction to interaction. Remember the principles you've already read in this book. Parents and teachers alike need to guard against common "misreactions."

- Avoid minimizing the problem. "Just ignore it."

- Don't rush to blame. "Well, what did you do to provoke him?"
- Resist immediately trying to fix the problem. "Just do this. . ."
- Avoid meddling when your child doesn't want your help. "We're going to go talk with those bullies' parents right now!"

This is one of the most difficult disciplines for parents. When my wife and I heard some of the things kids said about our son, we were livid. My wife was ready to fight a fifth-grade girl!

But we need to remember to turn our overreaction into interaction. Instead of rushing down to the school to talk with the principal and "fix it," start with empathy. By this I mean. . .

2. STEP INTO THEIR WORLD.

Almost every story in this book has one common denominator: an adult who didn't take the time to understand.

If you don't read anything else in this book, read this!

Step into your kid's world!

Earlier in the book I emphasized using your eyes and ears before your mouth. The key word I used was *empathy*—stepping into our kids' shoes and walking around in what they're experiencing. Instead of overreacting and making

STEP INTO YOUR KID'S WORLD!

them feel worse about an already embarrassing situation, slow down, watch, listen, and say, "I'm so glad you told me."

I can't repeat it enough. Your kids probably need a friend more than they need a solution. So step into their world, try your best to understand the living hell they're feeling, and "validate" what they're sharing.

"That must have been awful. Thanks so much for telling me."

It's nice when a victim of bullying has a friend their own age, but I'll be honest, most young people are lousy listeners. Adults can provide a mature listening ear that most young people lack. So open up those doors of communication.

In most of my interviews of bully victims, I asked the same final question: "When you're a parent, what will you do differently to help prevent your child from being bullied?"

Almost every person responded similarly:

- "I'd try to be more involved."
- "I'd listen more."
- "I'd believe my kid when they told me what happened."

Apparently we aren't doing a good enough job of noticing and listening. Don't underestimate the power of turning off your own screens and stepping into your kid's world.

Some parents will tell me, "Jonathan, I've tried this, and it's difficult to get them to open up."

If this is the case. . .

3. SEEK SETTINGS WHERE THEY OPEN UP.

One of the best ways to open the doors of dialogue is to look for settings where your kids seem to open up naturally.

When you put your kids to bed and their devices are all tuckered out and charging up their depleted batteries. . .at times like this, your kids might open up and communicate. It could start with a little question as you tuck them into bed.

"Mom? When you were my age, did anyone ever say something about you that wasn't true?"

Seek out venues where your kids seem more apt to open up. In fact, create these venues with simple guidelines like "no tech at the table." Who knows—every once in a while your kids might actually talk at the table.

If your son likes french fries at the greasy diner seven minutes from your house, poke your head in his room every once in a while and ask him, "Wanna go get some fries?"

If your daughter likes shoes (both of mine do), occasionally suggest, "Wanna go to the giant shoe outlet across from the mall and show me the next pair of shoes I can buy you?"

Sometimes it's not so much about the activity as about taking an interest in what they want to talk about. Enter their world. If you hear your kid talking about one of their favorite video games, ask them questions about it. If it's on their phone, you might say, "Cool, show me." Young people love being the expert. Allow them to show you the ropes of a world you don't know about.

Teachers can do this just the same. If you don't know much about an app, a social media platform, a musical artist, a Netflix show. . .ask them to educate you. You'll be surprised how much kids open up when you ask them to show you their world (again, not many people in their lives actually ask them about their world).

One of the school wellness counselors I interviewed told me how she counseled a kid who wasn't getting enough attention at home, so she connected with him through Minecraft. "I looked forward to what he crafted over the weekend and was able to affirm him for his creativity."

What venues, settings, and activities seem to entice your kids to share what's going on in their lives?

4. BE PROACTIVE ABOUT BUILDING IDENTITY.

Bullying is an attack on our kids' self-esteem. The roots of self-esteem sink deep into the question, "Who am I?"

BULLYING IS AN ATTACK ON OUR KIDS' SELF-ESTEEM.

It doesn't take long hearing descriptors like "loser" and "worthless" before you start believing them. Bullying can actually create PTSD-like symptoms. Common signs are feelings of worthlessness and helplessness, both of which feed anxiety.

We can help our kids develop a strong sense of self and, in turn, self-worth. One way to do this is by noticing their strengths and encouraging them in those strengths.

Every kid is good at something. It's your job to discover what it is.

My son, Alec, *wasn't* good at basketball or soccer, but he was creative and artsy and had an uncanny ability to impersonate others. He could watch a movie or cartoon once and then recite entire speeches word for word with perfect voice inflection.

Alec was nonstop entertainment!

Even if he was getting in trouble for sneaking a snack in the kitchen. My wife, Lori, would say, "Alec, what are you doing? You already had breakfast."

In a perfect Samwise Gamgee accent he would respond, "But this is second breakfast."

We always encouraged him. "Alec, you're so funny. Maybe you should take some drama classes," or "Maybe you could do those voices for cartoons!"

He actually went on to study art in college.

Affirm your kids in their natural gifting. But even more importantly, affirm them in their identity in Christ. That's one of the amazing things about putting your trust in Jesus. When we are "in Christ," we are a new creation (2 Corinthians 5:17). God molds us and makes us more like Him. We don't need to try to imitate others in this world; instead we let Christ transform us and renew our minds (Romans 12:1–2). This provides a healthy sense of self-worth.

Ask any therapist—confident kids know who they are and how they will present themselves to the world. Helping our kids develop "identity" helps them develop comfort with themselves.

If someone with strong self-esteem is teased for not being able to throw a football, they'll dismiss it. "I don't care if I can't throw a football. My worth isn't based on my athletic ability."

People with a strong sense of self are less targeted.

What is your kid good at?

How can you encourage them this week?

5. GIVE THEM A CHANCE TO SERVE.

Another way to help hurting kids feel valued is to give them the opportunity to help others.

I used to take middle school kids to my local food shelter to cook, clean, and serve food to the homeless. This experience was life-changing for many of these kids. Some of them were never given the opportunity to do something meaningful at home or school. Serving the needy often gives people an immediate sense of worth because they see the difference they're making right before their eyes.

You want a good remedy for depression?

Do something to help others.

Many times, when we step aside from our own struggles and help someone else, we realize our own struggles are minimal.

So give your kids an opportunity to serve and make a difference. It won't be a hard sell. This generation has grown up in a world where "giving back" is trendy. Every one of their celebrity role models is attached to some cause, helping homeless horses or saving sick salamanders. So give them a chance to do something meaningful.

Plus, service projects make a double impact: they give you an opportunity to do something charitable for someone else, and they also give you a sense of achievement when you complete a task.

Help the elderly with some yard work or housecleaning. I used to take kids window cleaning. I loved window cleaning because when you finish a job, you see the results of your labor. Kids would almost always say something like, "Look how clear those look! You can see *waaaay* better now." In fact, two of the young men I took with me eventually bought their own equipment and began cleaning windows for extra money. Now they were getting paid for a skill they had developed.

What are ways you can give your kids opportunities to serve?

What skills might they be able to develop and feel proud of?

6. BUILD CONFIDENCE AND CONNECTION.

I've seen a lot of parents enroll their kids in sports or drama, hoping these extracurricular activities will bring their kids out of their shell. But helping someone exhibiting antisocial behavior to become instantly social is a tricky (and often unsuccessful) undertaking. Resist the urge to just sign up your kid for soccer for the season. Instead, watch your kid and seek activities that have the potential to build confidence *and* connection.

What activities can you think of that might boost your child's self-confidence? Here are some thoughts:

- Do your best to find an activity they really enjoy and express an interest in. These activities aren't always readily apparent if all they do is sit at home and play video games. So give some activities a "tryout." Take them mountain biking or let them try out an art class. Some of these activities you might be able to do with them.

- Find activities that give them that sense of accomplishment we just talked about. Sometimes the bullied don't experience a lot of success or "wins" day to day. Provide opportunities that allow them to achieve something concrete and maybe even take pride in their work.

- Find a place where they can eventually be an expert. It doesn't matter if it's teaching Minecraft to kids two years younger. Give them a chance to use their skills to assist others. It's affirming.

- Find activities that make them feel more self-assured socially. Remember that bullied kids tend to remove themselves socially, which triggers a downward spiral toward isolation. Getting involved in activities where they experience successful social encounters can help them develop basic social skills. I knew a kid who started serving in a homeless shelter, which required him to talk with homeless people weekly. Over a period of six months, this kid found a new confidence in talking with others.

- Sometimes we can find athletic activities that boost their confidence physically. Maybe they aren't good at football but excel at wrestling. Sometimes kids aren't good at sports with a ball. Have they tried swimming or running? The Mayo clinic found that the psychological and physical benefits of exercise can help improve mood and reduce anxiety.[1] Not to mention, physical fitness might provide a little more confidence in situations where they need to respond in fight or flight.

Connection is a huge part of this equation. You've already learned that the best remedy against bullying is a friend, so seek out opportunities for your kids to socialize while doing activities they enjoy to increase the odds for them to meet someone with similar interests.

But be careful not to just "drop off" your child at karate or baseball practice. You might be dropping them into a den of lions. If your child has already experienced bullying in another setting, there's a good chance they might experience something similar in this new setting. So do a little research:

- Meet with the people involved, like teachers, coaches, or instructors, and subtly ask them about the other kids there. "Are there other kids who also wear a Batman mask to bed and love origami?"
- Watch your child the first time you bring them and notice if they connect with other kids. More importantly, notice if the other kids are being mean. Do your best not to be or even appear like that creepy stalker parent who meddles in everything their kid does. See if there is a way you can observe quietly and inconspicuously (all your kid needs now is to be labeled a "mama's boy"). If there's no way to watch your child without drawing attention to yourself, then skip this part and trust the adult you already "interviewed."

I can't overemphasize the importance of socialization. Reread the section about the impact of "one friend" in chapter 8 if you must. The research is compelling and undeniable. Friends make a huge difference. Social connection is extremely therapeutic for bullied kids.

Who knows—that painting club, karate class, or church youth group might be the place they meet their best friend.

Where are some places your kids might build confidence and connect with others like them?

What can you do this week to initiate that connection?

7. DODGE DANGER ZONES.

If your kid isn't athletic, then don't drop them off at wrestling camp in hopes that it's a cure-all. Don't get me wrong—wrestling camp might be just what your kid needs. That's why you need to get to know your kid, listen to their experiences, empathize with their struggles, hear their complaints, watch them socially, and then—and only then—help them pick some positive activities.

Let's stop and consider some of the places that might be a little extra difficult for someone who gets picked on more than others. Think of the stories you've been reading so far. Does your twelve-year-old really need that Instagram account (which they're not even supposed to have)?

Does your kid need to walk home alone from school?

I'm not encouraging you to turn into a helicopter parent and swoop down to save your kid every time they encounter something difficult. Far from it. Continue to give them practical experience doing chores, meeting real people (service projects give them both those opportunities), and handling real-world problems. But avoid sending them into arenas that set them up for failure.

Here are some common arenas where a lot of bullying takes place:

- *The school bus or bus stop.* If your child is experiencing bullying, see if there is any way you can avoid sending them to school on a big yellow school bus. I don't think I've ever been on a school bus that *didn't* have a bully on it.
- *The locker room.* If your child doesn't have to take any

more physical education courses, then don't make them take any. Not because of the course. . .because of the locker rooms! Locker rooms are full of bullies (both guys' and girls' locker rooms!).

- *Social media.* I pounded this point earlier in the book, and I'll emphasize it again. Delay social media as long as possible. Kids aren't even supposed to be on it until age thirteen (COPPA), and even then parents should only subject them to it if they are proving to be responsible in that area. If you see them obsessing over their lack of friends on Instagram, that is not being responsible.

As a side note, I'd like to mention that parents of bystanders (and of bullies) can help out bullied kids by offering their kids some accountability online. Some helpful software applications are available that provide families with what I call "transparency." If sister downloads an app, then mom and dad see what she just downloaded. If brother makes a rude comment on social media, then everyone sees that comment.

Wouldn't it be nice if most parents were aware of what their kids were posting on social media?

A few years ago fifteen-year-old tech whiz Trisha Prabhu created an app to help prevent cyberbullying. Her app, ReThink, detects when someone tries to post something offensive on social media, alerting them and asking them, "Are you sure you want to post that?"[2]

Social media is today's most dangerous playground where bullies thrive. Avoid danger zones like this as much as possible.

What are the danger zones your child might be exposed to?

What adjustments can you make?

8. TEACH GOOD SOCIAL SKILLS.

A great way to help socially awkward kids is to teach them social skills, problem-solving, conflict management, and assertiveness.

Scratch that. *All kids* need to know these skills!

This could be as simple as doing what we keep talking about in this chapter: involving them in social activities they actually enjoy and giving them real-world practice at having conversations with peers each day. But sometimes it also might entail giving them some moderate coaching on social behaviors. Teach your child listening skills and how to ask questions. Affirm them when you see them making an effort. Be proactive about catching them doing something right. And yes, gently correct them when you see them engaging in antisocial behaviors.

"Justin, your brother just let you borrow his Dwayne 'The Rock' Johnson Power Doll with Pulsating Pectorals. What do you say?"

Problem-solving and conflict management are skills most young people are void of today. I was just talking with someone in youth ministry about this quandary. We're raising a generation of kids who hide under headphones blaring music affirming their "right" to gun down anyone who disrespects them (literally).[3] We need to teach this generation how to solve conflict, and the best coaches are Mom and Dad.

This might include teaching our kids how to stick up for themselves and what that looks like. Opinions vary on this subject, and I definitely don't want to advise you to teach your kids to solve their problems with violence. I'll just say it like this: many experts are big believers in teaching our kids how to stand up for themselves.

The good news is that much of this is mental. Confident kids who "know who they are" are less likely to be picked on in the first place. But sometimes kids are backed into a corner. . .literally. It's good when Mom or Dad has spent some time talking with them about what to do in these situations.

And the best way to teach our kids how to resolve conflict?

Model it.

No pressure, Mom and Dad.

Which leads me to my last two tools to help hurting kids. . .

9. TEACH FORGIVENESS.

Bullying is a unique kind of hurt. My heart breaks when I recall the different testimonies I've written about in this book, where people say things like, "There are people I hate, and I haven't seen them in fifteen years."

There's only one cure for this kind of bitterness.

Forgiveness.

When we hold on to hate, all we are doing is locking ourselves in a prison cell of our own bitterness.

BULLYING IS A UNIQUE KIND OF HURT.

We can provide our kids with the key to unlock that prison of bitterness and hate.

Teach forgiveness the same way you teach anything to young people. Don't say, "You need to do this." Just present the truth and let them form their own conclusion.

Read stories like the "parable of the unmerciful servant" in the Bible (Matthew 18:21–35). Then ask questions:

- "How do you think the servant felt when the king forgave his huge debt?"
- "Why do you think he wasn't the same way with his own servants?"
- "What point was Jesus making?"
- "What is one thing we can do this week to live out the moral of this parable?"

Or read the story of Jesus Himself being mocked, tortured, and crucified on the cross, only to cry out, "Father, forgive them, for they do not know what they are doing."

And again, the best way to teach forgiveness is to model it in our own lives.

Are you holding on to any grudges that you need to give to God?

Are you locking yourself in a prison cell of bitterness?

I've been there.

There's only one cure, and it's not anything from human power. The cure is simply to give up and cry out to God, "God, I can't do it on my own. I need Your strength to forgive."

That moment of weakness will give you the power. It's not yours, but it's power far greater than you could ever come up with on your own.

Share this life-changing truth with your kids.

10. GET SUPPORT YOURSELF.

It's difficult to help our kids when our own lives are a mess. I know when our son, Alec, started being picked on, it wrecked us!

Parents need community just as much as our kids do. If you're dealing with a kid who's hurting, reach out to others for prayer and emotional support.

One of the moms I talked with was dealing with a painful situation in which her daughter was being targeted on social media. This mom went to an ironic location for support—social media. She reached out to her Facebook friends and asked for prayer and guidance. She was inundated with love and support from friends, stories of encouragement, and listening ears. She told me, "I don't know if we would have made it without our community gathering around us."

My family experienced this need to depend on others firsthand. When Alec entered fifth grade, the bullying became worse and worse. It was a daily battle, and Lori and I were pulling our hair out. I was pretty close to reacting in some unhealthy ways.

We reached out to some friends for prayer, and we were showered with support. Funny thing, that support actually provided me with some accountability. When I had thirty friends asking me, "How's it going?" I knew it wouldn't be good to say, "Well, I got arrested for beating up another dad today."

Don't hesitate to surround yourself with community in tough times like this.

Where can you go for support?

Is there a church, home group, or Bible study group in your community you might want to join?

Think of the stories you've heard throughout this book. Recall statements like, "No one cared," "No one listened," "They didn't do a thing."

Sadly, our world is full of parents, teachers, and administrators who are so preoccupied or overwhelmed with their own world that they are ignoring kids' cries of hurt.

But not you.

The fact that you're reading this tells me you have your eyes open for the warning signs, you're willing to listen, and you're willing to do whatever it takes to help that struggling kid you care about so much. . .even if it means meeting with the school or another set of parents.

Let's talk about how to do that.

SADLY, OUR WORLD IS FULL OF PARENTS, TEACHERS, AND ADMINISTRATORS WHO ARE SO PREOCCUPIED OR OVERWHELMED WITH THEIR OWN WORLD THAT THEY ARE IGNORING KIDS' CRIES OF HURT.

DISCUSSION QUESTIONS

1. What was one thing in this chapter that really stood out to you?

2. What checks and balances can you put into place to avoid "freaking out" and making the situation worse?

3. What is a venue where your kids seem to open up the most?

4. What are your kids good at? How can you encourage them in those skills this week?

5. What activities might be good for your kids, helping them build confidence and/or connection?

6. How can you teach your kids to forgive. . .especially those who are difficult to love and forgive?

7. How can you model love and forgiveness this week?

CHAPTER 11
MEET THE PRINCIPAL / MEET THE PARENTS
"Hello, my child is being bullied."

If an elephant has its foot on the tail of a mouse,
and you say that you are neutral, the mouse
will not appreciate your neutrality.
–Desmond Tutu

"Hello, I'm the parent of Michael, and he's being bullied by Brayden!"

Most of the bullying stories in the interviews I conducted included a pinnacle moment where mom and/or dad contacted the teacher, the principal, or the parents of the other kids involved. In the overwhelming majority of the stories, that meeting didn't go well. In fact, the words I heard most were: "It only made the problem worse."

Why?

Are principals too busy to deal with kids who don't play well with others?

Do parents of bullies have their heads buried in the sand?

Or is there a chance that parents of bullying victims are typically irrational at the moment?

Could it also have to do with the mere nature of a bully—bullies are angered and only provoked more when you involve the authorities?

IS THIS JUST AN IMPOSSIBLE SITUATION, OR CAN PARENTS AND SCHOOL ADMINISTRATORS ACTUALLY PARTNER TO MAKE SCHOOL (AND AFTER SCHOOL) A SAFE PLACE FOR EVERYONE?

Is this just an impossible situation, or can parents and school administrators actually partner to make school (and after school) a safe place for everyone?

TWO SIDES

There are two sides to every story.

As I interviewed the parents of children who had been the target of bullying and then the kids themselves, one of the recurrent phrases I heard was, "The school did little to fix the problem."

Yet in my interviews with principals, teachers, and other school administrators, I kept hearing about parents who were accusative and unreasonable. One vice principal told me, "Often moms are so emotional about what happened, they are completely irrational." I even had a female school administrator tell me, "I prefer working with dads. They are so much more black and white." (Her words, not mine.)

It's intriguing hearing both sides.

Obviously I understand the parents' perspective. I was bullied mercilessly and felt like teachers did nothing. My own son was targeted by his entire fifth-grade class, and the principal did literally nothing to help the situation. These experiences probably even impede my objectivity in the matter. I would be excused from a jury immediately on any case involving bullying.

But having worked alongside teachers and principals for the last few decades, and having countless friends and family members who are teachers (my mom was a teacher, my sister-in-law is a teacher, my daughter is subbing right now and getting her credentials), I sympathize with their position. It's not easy being a leader. Caring for young people is no easy task.

So why do these meetings often fall short of expectations on one or both sides?

Let's look at both perspectives; then I'd like to offer some humble advice to each side.

FROM THE PRINCIPAL'S DESK

Often principals don't hear from parents unless there's a problem. They could be doing ninety-eight things right, but as soon as a problem erupts, they'll have eight angry parents sitting in the waiting room.

This is understandable. Who has time to schedule a meeting with the principal just to tell her, "You're doing a great job! I love the way you are present on campus and know my kid's name."

Principals probably wouldn't even want hundreds of parents coming in just to say, "Thanks!" (Although they probably wouldn't mind a nice note telling them exactly that.)

At times the principal and vice principal's job is kind of like the job of the poor lady at the customer service counter at an airport: all she does is deal with problems. All day long she interacts with angry people who are stressed out of their minds because they just missed their flight to Orlando.

From what I've observed, many parents whose kids are experiencing bullying tend to enter the situation in blame mode.

"What are you going to do about this?!"

"How could you let this happen on your watch?"

Every administrator I spoke with discussed the struggle they felt because they legally are not allowed to reveal to parents facts about other kids. This handcuffs them in some ways. They would love to tell you, "I met with the little punk and suspended him for a year!" But they can't tell you that. It's a catch-22: while parents want to be able to have a certain level of trust in the administration, they often feel their trust has not been earned.

Parents also tend to enter the situation emotionally. I understand this completely. It's hard not to be emotional when you see your child suffering. My wife and I were both basket cases.

But sometimes *emotional* overpowers *rational*. So now a principal has to deal with someone who honestly isn't thinking logically. Many parents are blinded by anger as they enter the principal's office and haven't even considered anyone else's perspective—or the chance that they might be getting only part of the story from their own kid.

I know, I know. For parents of a kid who is being targeted, this possibility might be difficult to consider. Remember, I know your perspective well. But looking back, I've come to realize there were things I didn't know and some assumptions I made that kept me from dealing with certain situations fairly.

Please consider the following ideas when approaching that principal, vice principal, or teacher:

SIX TIPS FOR PARENTS PREPARING TO MEET WITH THE PRINCIPAL OR TEACHER

1. PAUSE.

No meeting is so urgent that it requires you to walk in out of control.

Go on a run, a walk, a bike ride. . .whatever it takes to clear your head. Pray. Call up a friend and rant. Find a corner booth at your favorite Mexican restaurant and eat three bowls of chips (okay, I think I just confessed what I do). Just do something to get your senses about you so you don't go into an important meeting like this emotionally wrecked.

I recently finished studying the book of Esther. This little book of the Bible offers a fascinating perspective on "pause." The king pronounced an edict "to destroy, kill and annihilate all the Jews—young and old, women and children—on a single day" (Esther 3:13). The king's wife, Esther, a Jew, was "in great distress" (Esther 4:4).

So what did she do?

She paused for three days. In fact, she encouraged everyone to do the same:

> *"Go, gather together all the Jews who are in Susa, and fast for me. Do not eat or drink for three days, night or day. I and my attendants will fast as you do. When this is done, I will go to the king, even though it is against the law. And if I perish, I perish."* (Esther 4:16)

If you read the rest of the story, you'll be amazed what God does. After those three days, God orchestrated a series of events that changed the whole course of the book. . .all because Esther paused.

It's never good to walk into an already volatile situation with only half your wits.

My friend Kim is a dean at a private school. She told me of times when parents came in so flustered that she needed to ask them to go home and calm down so they could simply talk.

"Try to be non-emotional," Kim advised. "Use non-feeling words. Share the facts."

Which brings me to my next tip for parents. . .

2. RECOGNIZE PERCEIVED VERSUS ACTUAL.

Sometimes when parents are emotional, they tend to generalize or even exaggerate.

"My daughter is being targeted by the entire school!"

Really? The *entire* school?

I remember when my son, Alec, was being targeted by a large group of bullies in his class. To him it felt like literally everyone.

Alec would walk around by himself during recess wishing someone would play with him. Even his one friend, Aidan, abandoned Alec once he realized a friendship with Alec would probably mean he'd be bullied too.

For us, it felt like "everyone" was against him. In hindsight, there were a few bullies and an excess of spineless bystanders.

If your kid is in this situation, describe the actual situation:

> A group of about seven or eight girls are making fun of my daughter Addison at school and on social media. Here's a printout of some of the posts. Even though it's only about seven or eight of them who are aggressively and repetitively mocking her, many of her classmates are laughing and joining in. For example, earlier this week when Chloe posted this picture of Addison's face on a gorilla's body during fifth-period algebra, in addition to the seven or eight of those girls in her class, many of the other students in the class began making sounds like a monkey—Abigail and Emily, who have never said anything mean in the past, actually offered her a banana.

This kind of description is far more convincing than "Everyone hates my daughter!"

Collecting actual facts can be difficult for parents because sometimes we are hearing the stories secondhand, and at times our kids describe what they "perceive" more than what is "actually" happening.

That's why it's important not to rush this process. Part of empathetic listening is asking our kids how they feel. After we've done what we've talked about so much already in this book, making our kids feel noticed and heard, and resisting the urge to fix the situation right away, we eventually need to draw out some facts, maybe even in a separate conversation in which we ask, "Give me some specific examples of what you're experiencing so I can better understand."

Document. If there is proof, like texts or screenshots, collect those. Slowly collect the facts you need to rationally present actual events that occurred. If all you have is firsthand testimony, then that's what you'll need to present:

> Sean told me that this week in the cafeteria Gavin and Dylan knocked his lunch tray out of his hands. As a result, Sean didn't eat that day, but he seemed more shook up about the fact that so many of his classmates were laughing when it happened. This is the third time this has happened this month. His friends Seth and Jackson were there all three times.

Share the facts. Principals and teachers will appreciate having actual facts to work with. Feelings don't always help the situation.

3. BE OPEN TO THE POSSIBILITY THAT YOUR KID MIGHT NOT BE INNOCENT.

I'm not suggesting you victimize your kid, considering her guilty until proven innocent. I'm just recommending you keep an open mind as you're gathering information. Sometimes things aren't what they seem.

My friends who are teachers and administrators joke that the most common response from parents is, "Not my kid." You might know that well, because if you've ever confronted another parent about their child bullying your child, they probably responded, "What? My little Britney?"

Sorry, Mom, haven't you heard? Britney's not that innocent.

My friend Michelle, who works at a school, recounted a time when another parent called her up and accused Michelle's son of stealing her son's history book, crossing out his name, and putting his own name in its place. Michelle felt the words "Not my kid" almost leave her lips, but she had heard those words from parents far too many times. So she talked with her son later that night.

"I got a call from Andrew's mom today about his history book. Is there anything I should know?"

That was all that needed to be said. He confessed to everything, and it was exactly as Andrew's mom described.

I've witnessed stories of kids who claimed, "I was bullied," when in fact that was the furthest thing from the truth. One girl who had a hard time making friends decided to bang her head against the bathroom wall until she passed out. She claimed "bully" and had a lengthy story ready. The truth eventually came out.

That's why these situations take time and patience. When our kids cry "bully," we need to listen first and resist the urge to victimize or blame. But this doesn't mean wearing a blindfold. We still need to seek the truth. Sometimes the truth isn't exactly what our kids—even our bullied kids—present.

Humility is always a good approach when you meet with the principal or teacher.

4. KNOW WHAT YOU WANT.

Know what your goal is for the meeting. Don't just present a bunch of facts and hope that the principal or teacher knows exactly what to do. Make a specific request.

Here are some reasonable requests and questions from parents:

- Can I have these parents' phone numbers so I can contact them and talk this situation through with them?

- What is your bullying protocol?
- What is a fair expectation for how this situation will be handled?
- Can you please *not* talk with the other kids yet, but simply observe the situation and see what you notice?

That last example is so important I want to highlight it as a separate tip.

5. ASK FOR OBSERVATION INSTEAD OF CONFRONTATION.

One of the biggest complaints I heard from both kids and parents was when the school administration called the bullies and the bullied together in one room to try to work it out. So be clear if that is *not* what you want.

Instead, ask the principal or teacher to just watch and see what they observe.

How many times have you heard me tell a story in this book about a lack of adult presence in the locker room, hallway, or cafeteria? Maybe the school administration could use a humble nudge to "watch" what goes on in the cafeteria and on the playground.

If our kids are telling us the truth, observation will be all the revelation you need.

Sure, some adults aren't very sly about watching sensitive situations like this. But usually if a teacher or principal is made aware of potential bullying, the increased adult presence and watchful eyes can decrease the frequency of the bullying. If the bullying continues when adults are *not* watching, you obviously can schedule another meeting where you bring in new information about where and when so they can be proactive about looking for it.

If the bullying is happening on social media during the night, then a printout of the mean posts is all you need. And honestly, the principal isn't necessarily the one who needs to solve that. You might need to. . .

6. MEET THE PARENTS.

One of my friends who is a school administrator told me, "The biggest problem of bullying we have on campus doesn't even occur on campus! It occurs on social media the night before! But parents think it's our job to solve it."

If your daughter's soccer teammates post mean stuff about her, it's a good idea to go directly to their parents. Don't do this unless you've already listened to your daughter and made her feel noticed and heard, *and* she asked for your help. I heard numerous testimonies from kids who said their parents intervened and made the situation worse.

"Do you think your mommy can save you?"

Conversely, I heard just as many share how they wish their mom and dad would have done something, but they didn't. The only way to discover how your kid would like you to help is by being there for them.

What if your kid needs your help but doesn't want it?

Do your best to equip your child with the tools they need to solve the situation by themselves. But if the situation doesn't get any better, then it's your job as a parent to step in.

Don't expect an eight-, ten-, or twelve-year-old to know what's best. Sometimes you need to step in and meet the parents of the other kids involved.

If you don't know their parents, ask the school for their contact information.

When meeting with parents, remember some of these same tips:

- *Pause.* Don't go knocking on some other mom's door ready to start a fight. Take some time not only to calm down but also to think through the best way to confront the issue.
- *Recognize perceived versus actual.* Don't go making generalizations or wild accusations. You're addressing Mama Bear about her cubs. Chances are if you show her a printout of her daughter's social media feed mocking your daughter, she still might defend

her. So be prepared to calmly and rationally present facts that she can ponder.

- *Ask questions and let them draw the conclusions.* Instead of saying, "Your evil little daughter posted this," try asking, "I didn't really know how to react to this. Is this Instagram post from your daughter?"
- *Give them time to think.* Don't expect them to have the perfect response. Give them the facts to chew on and the time to digest.
- *End with a request to reconvene.* Humbly ask them if they'd like to talk with their kid, hear their side of the story, and then meet together again to come up with a way to resolve the situation.

Hopefully parents will receive this gentle confrontation with an open mind, as opposed to "Not my kid!" Many times their reaction will depend on how the accusation is presented.

But parents aren't the only ones with a stake in these situations. Teachers and principals also have a responsibility to address issues of bullying.

TIPS FOR PRINCIPALS AND TEACHERS

The last chapter of this book is devoted to what schools can do to break through the problem of bullying, so I don't want to jump the gun, but here are a handful of quick tips that principals and teachers can consider specifically when parents or kids meet with you about bullying.

1. EMPATHIZE.

It's difficult to stop and be a counselor for one kid when you're responsible for countless others. But the best way to help not only the student but also the parents feel noticed and heard is to empathize.

Ask them what they've experienced. Maybe even offer a compassionate response like, "I'm sorry that happened."

Parents will appreciate this.

Bullied kids *need* this.

You won't lose your position of disciplinarian if you later find out their story was all a lie.

What is the downside of offering all kids—even the bullies—the presumption of innocence?

Which leads me to my second tip. . .

2. DON'T VICTIMIZE EVERYONE.

Sure, you don't know everyone's side of the story yet. But what if the kid sitting in front of you is truly an innocent victim of bullying? Have you already treated them like a criminal?

When you called them in to meet with you, did they have to sit in a waiting room where other students could see them? You know what kids do when they see a kid waiting for the principal.

"Oooh, busted!"

If you brought all the parties involved into the room, did you treat them all like they were guilty until proven innocent? I didn't type that wrong. If a kid is bullied at your school, do they have to go through a trial to prove they're not just some kid in a random fight?

Sorting out the facts might take time. That's why you'll need to. . .

3. BE OPEN TO IT TAKING MORE THAN ONE MEETING.

In my research, the typical response from schools was to call all the kids into the same room, ask for everyone's side of the story, then make everyone shake hands and promise to play nice.

Bada boom, bada bing!

Is there a chance it's not that simple?

I know you're busy and you'd like to get this situation checked off your list, but consider what the families are going through.

Often it's difficult to discern the truth in one meeting if you have no context or history observing the situation. It's completely reasonable to listen and collect information during the first meeting, assure them you will personally observe the situation, and then set the next meeting on all of your calendars right then.

Eliminate the possibility of parents saying, "I never heard from her again!"

The second meeting also places a little pressure on you to actually do what you said: observe the situation.

4. TAKE TIME TO OBSERVE.

Watch the situation for a while. Talk with teachers or yard duty volunteers and ask them to keep a sly eye on the kids involved. Do some recon to find the truth of the matter.

Remember that *bullies* are often smooth socially and get along with adults well, whereas *the bullied* are often awkward and withdrawn. So be careful judging what you see sitting in the chairs in front of you at face value. The smooth-talking, rational kid might be the guilty one, and the frustrating kid making unreasonable outbursts just might be the one who is being targeted by Eddie Haskell sitting next to him.

Watch the smooth kid when he doesn't know he's being watched. Watch how he treats the awkward kid when he's *not* in your office.

5. HELP THE PARENTS WITH CLOSURE.

Sure, there are facts you cannot disclose. But you can at least call up the parents and say, "I met with the parties involved, we found validity to many of your child's claims, and several of the students involved were punished. Furthermore, we are going to continue watching the situation carefully."

Maybe parents do want to know more. Maybe they want to hear that you hung up the bullies by their toes. But any reasonable parent would be happy just hearing that you actually followed through. That would have made me happy.

Parents, teachers, and principals typically all want the same thing in these situations: the truth. The key is partnering together to discover it. Hopefully these tips help in that process.

Be prepared: Some people are just difficult. At times you will do everything right and still receive a bad response.

Sadly, many of the stories I heard ended with the statement, "So we finally switched schools and that solved the problem." Sometimes that's what it takes, though hopefully it doesn't come to that.

PARENTS, TEACHERS, AND PRINCIPALS TYPICALLY ALL WANT THE SAME THING IN THESE SITUATIONS: THE TRUTH.

DISCUSSION QUESTIONS

1. What was one thing in this chapter that really stood out to you?

2. Why do you think so many of the parents Jonathan interviewed didn't have positive experiences with their kid's school?

3. Why do you think so many of the principals, teachers, and administrators Jonathan interviewed didn't have positive experiences with parents?

4. Which to you is the most helpful of Jonathan's six tips for parents preparing to meet with a principal?

5. Which tip for meeting the parents of a bully do you think is most helpful?

6. Which tip for principals and teachers do you think they need to hear the most?

7. If you are a principal or teacher, which tip do you think you need to hear the most?

8. What is one thing you can do this week to partner together as parents and administration to make school a safe place for our kids?

CHAPTER 12
SCHOOL SHOOTINGS
Pushed beyond the tipping point

My pain may be the reason for somebody's laugh.
But my laugh must never be the reason for somebody's pain.
–Charlie Chaplin

Do you remember where you were April 20, 1999?

Each generation has a date like this they recollect. For my parents it was the day John F. Kennedy was shot. For my grandparents it was Pearl Harbor. For my kids it was 9/11.

For me it was Columbine.

April 20, 1999, was a Tuesday, and I was with my five-year-old at his swim practice. I was twenty-nine years old and had been in youth ministry for almost a decade. My coworker Don called me on my cell phone.

"Are you near a TV?" he asked, obviously shaken up.

"No," I said. "Why?"

He began detailing the events he was watching on the news, kids soaked in blood being lowered out of windows, SWAT team members escorting lines of frightened teenagers to safety, interviews with panic-stricken parents.

Time revealed that two students brought guns and bombs to school that day to act out some sort of revenge. Thirteen were killed, many more injured. And then we began to hear the word:

Bullied.

Bullying has become a significant contributing factor to countless acts of revenge on campus. Like the story of Alicia Graham.

Sound familiar?

Of course not.

Even if you studied school shootings, you wouldn't recognize this name. . .by a few degrees of separation anyway.

Alicia Graham was targeted by a group of bullies at her high school, Franklin Regional High School in Murrysville, Pennsylvania, who taunted her frequently on social media.

"That's how it is at Franklin," Alicia said. "Everybody bullies everybody."

Alicia's dad printed out a list of the texts and cruel posts and brought them to the school, including a list of her tormentors.

"I felt like they kind of waved a gold wand over it," he said, explaining that it was an affluent community. (Sadly, I keep hearing this again and again from parents whose kids were bullied.)

The problem didn't go away. Alicia was still tormented by her aggressors. In fact, a few months later Alicia was attacked by a girl in the school cafeteria who hit her with a lunch tray and beat her until a teacher pulled the girl off of her. Alicia suffered a concussion and missed three days of school.

As for the list of tormentors?

It didn't stop them.

Several months later, one of Alicia's same tormentors posted something cruel on social media about another kid at the school, a quiet, shy kid named Alex Hribal.

Does that name sound familiar?

The next day, Alex took two knives to school, slashing the arms and faces of fellow students and stabbing people in the torso, leaving a total of twenty-one victims at Franklin Regional High.[1]

Am I implying that this one cruel social media post was the cause of the Franklin High School stabbing?

No. In fact, a lengthy manifesto was found in Hribal's locker blaming other students for being cruel to him and actually praising Eric Harris and Dylan Klebold for their actions at Columbine back in 1999.[2]

Hribal was obviously a very disturbed young man whose actions are horrifying and unconscionable. Klebold, Harris. . .the whole list. . .reprehensible. Their actions inexcusable.

But what of the students who ridiculed these kids?[3]

And what about the administrators who let these kinds of

activities continue under their watch?

THE BOY WHO CRIED, "BULLY."

Bully has become almost a buzzword. Whenever a school shooting happens, you're almost waiting for it.

The media sticks a microphone in a random kid's face. "Was this kid bullied?"

"I'm not sure. I think so!"

Good enough. "He was bullied!"

The shooter's defense attorney immediately begins laying the groundwork for his case. "It was bullying that drove him to act out."

Bullying has become a go-to excuse for acts of violence like these.

Is there any truth to these claims?

Are many of the school shootings we keep seeing on the news a result of bullying?

It's difficult to blame one cause for every senseless act of violence on campus. In many cases the shooters are killed and no one really knows why they did what they did. Some skeptics think bullying *isn't* the problem.

"It's mental illness that needs to be addressed."

"Gun legislation is the problem!"

Even when students claim bullying, people aren't always convinced. When Caleb Sharpe gunned down a classmate and wounded others at a Washington state high school, he actually told police he wanted to "teach everyone a lesson about what happens when you bully others."[4]

Some claimed Sharpe's answer was too simplistic. One of his classmates described him as "pretty mentally unstable" and "pretty interested in violence." A "school shooting expert" said, "Instead of asking if someone was bullied, it's important to take a broader view. The shooter's mental health, home life, and school life all need to be considered."[5]

This same expert claims he has studied dozens of school shootings and that they are rarely precipitated by bullying. He tried to support his statement by showing that only four of eighty-three intended victims of school shooters he studied were actually bullies.

I'm sorry, but I'm going on the record to say that I completely disagree with this "expert's" claim that school shootings are rarely precipitated by bullying. What about the bystanders who laughed every time these kids were teased? In the eyes of the bullied, they are guilty by association.

I might mention as an aside that I've done over one hundred hours of research into school shootings, written a novel about one, and personally interviewed Columbine victims. . .and I don't call myself an expert.

Let me just say this. Yes, mental illness and home life are huge factors. I'd call "home life" monumental, actually.

But I had an amazing home life. And I can tell you, if I had access to a gun in junior high, I would have considered blowing away not only the entire "Kill Jon Club" but every one of the smug bystanders who laughed at their jokes and T-shirts! (Wow, did I just put that in print?) By God's grace, I never did. But take it from me: public ridicule does something to you mentally. It festers and boils, becoming something poisonous.

Maybe what I'm actually corroborating is his statement, "The shooter's mental health, home life, and school life all need to be considered." Because even if your mental health and your home life are good, if you are being targeted by your peers every day, it does something to you. It doesn't have to be a mix of all these factors. That one factor alone just might be enough—your school life. It absolutely can change your mental health quickly.

I've got two words of proof for you: Dylan Klebold.

PUSHED TOO FAR

I've read every police report and watched almost every video on record of Columbine's Eric Harris and Dylan Klebold. In my opinion, Harris might have had some serious mental issues. But not many had anything bad to say about his home life, even Eric himself. In fact, one day Eric was doodling in his school planner. He wrote a quotation from *The Tempest*: "Good wombs have borne bad sons."

Eric wrote this on the day marked "Mother's Day."

So if we were to create some checkboxes for Eric Harris, they might look like this:

> Poor mental health   ✓
> Bad home life
> Rough school life   ✓

But what about Dylan Klebold?

Dylan showed no signs of mental illness, and every source shows he was from a very loving home.

So what pushed him over the edge?

Dylan wasn't prom king. He wasn't a jock. He was nerdy and loved video games. And he was a follower. Sadly, he started following a very bitter, sick young man named Eric.

What linked him with Eric?

They both were bullied by the same group at school.

> Poor mental health
> Bad home life
> Rough school life   ✓

Bullying was a huge problem at Columbine. Even our school shooting expert couldn't deny that.

I'm not going to start naming names, but a quick Google search will reveal countless articles about some of the "white-hatted" bullies at Columbine, a tough group of jocks who used to mock and intimidate anyone who didn't measure up to their pathetic criteria.

A young man named Jonathan Greene experienced extreme bullying from a couple of "white hats" on the wrestling team. They used to actually pin him on the ground and give him "body twisters." "He got bruises all over his body," his dad recalled.[6]

Jonathan was Jewish. In gym class they hurled racial slurs about him, literally singing songs about Hitler and yelling out, "Another Jew in the oven." The gym teacher, who was also the school's wrestling coach, did nothing.

When Greene's dad went to the wrestling coach and the guidance counselor, they told him, "This stuff can happen."

Greene's dad wasn't having it. So he called the school board, which notified the police. The two athletes were charged and sentenced to probation. But both were allowed to continue football and wrestling.

Another one of the "white hats" began teasing a classmate about her breasts. When she went to her teacher, who was also a football and wrestling coach, he suggested she move to another seat.

Did you ever wonder why when Harris and Klebold started shooting they yelled, "All the jocks stand up. Anybody with a white hat or a shirt with a sports emblem on it is dead."

Perhaps bullying had a bigger effect on these two than many of the "experts" realized.

On YouTube if you search for "Columbine basement tapes," you'll find a series of videos the two boys made just months before the massacre. Most of these videos have a common theme: revenge against bullies.

In these little video skits, a friend would say, "People are always making fun of me. I don't like it. I need some help!" Then two boys dressed in trench coats would arrive on the scene to offer protection. You can watch take after take of Dylan yelling rants like, "Do not mess with that friggin' kid. If you do, I'll rip off your G*dd**n head and. . ."; then he would laugh between takes.

Dylan didn't have a history of bitterness or hate. . .until he began experiencing bullying. . .and until he found camaraderie with Harris.

Harris had all kinds of bottled-up aggression. Police had even been tipped off to his website, which read: "I will rig up explosives all over a town and detonate each one of them at will after I mow down a whole area of you snotty rich [expletives]. . . . All I want to do is kill and injure as many of you as I can."[7]

So are school shooters like Harris and Klebold unique? What about Sharpe? Hribal? Or Florida Parkland shooter Nikolas Cruz, whom classmates identified as being bullied every day? Are we seeing a pattern? Does bullying increase the chances of a kid using weapons and violence to solve their problems?

What influences a kid to bring a weapon to school?

The journal *Pediatrics* recently conducted a fascinating study in which they observed the likelihood of a student bringing a weapon to school. In their survey of American high school students, they found over 20 percent reported being a victim of bullying in the last year, and over 4 percent reported carrying a weapon to school.[8]

But the study really gets intriguing when additional risk factors are thrown into the mix. For example, when victims of bullying experienced three additional risk factors, like fighting at school, being threatened or injured at school, and/or skipping school out of fear for their safety, they were far more likely to bring a weapon to school. In fact, the subset of victims of bullying who had these three additional adverse experiences had a 46.4 percent likelihood of carrying weapons to school compared with just 2.5 percent for nonvictims.

Look at those numbers again and let that sink in for a moment.

Perhaps schools might want to develop some simple checkboxes for these risk factors?

I'm not here to cast stones or point fingers. Like you, I want solutions. And schools would be foolish to ignore studies like this revealing the "perfect storm" effect these multiple factors have on a kid's mental health.

Schools, do you keep records of fights, threats, and skipping school? What if we put these factors into a database that trips an alarm as soon as two or more happen?

BULLYING DOESN'T TYPICALLY RESOLVE ITSELF. IT CAN'T BE IGNORED.

Bullying doesn't typically resolve itself.

It can't be ignored.

Sadly, when it is, some kids are pushed beyond the tipping point.

The last words of Sam Strahan before fifteen-year-old Caleb Sharpe shot him were, "I always knew you were going to shoot up the school."[9]

So why didn't he say something?

Maybe no one was listening.

How can schools listen and respond? Let's take a look in the next chapter.

DISCUSSION QUESTIONS

1. What was one thing in this chapter that really stood out to you?

2. What were you doing when Columbine happened?

3. Do you think Columbine would have happened if there were no bullies at the school?

4. Why do you think Columbine teachers and coaches seemed so quick to look the other way?

5. How can schools do a better job of noticing incidents of bullying?

6. How can we all do a better job of noticing when a kid is being pushed toward the tipping point?

7. What is one thing you can do this week to proactively seek out isolated and ostracized kids?

CHAPTER 13
LOCKER ROOMS AND HALLWAYS
Seven tools that actually help schools

Doug is the principal of a suburban, six-hundred-kid middle school not fifteen minutes from my house. It's the only school in the entire Sacramento area that insists "every kid" participate in an all-day antibullying event called "Point Break."[1] About fifty campuses in the area have done the event, but most send only select kids.

Doug sends *every* seventh grader. By the time a kid graduates, they've attended the program.

The purpose of Point Break is to improve the values, attitudes, and behaviors of high school students on their campuses and in their communities, intervening *before* acts of bullying, hatred, or violence occur.

I attended one of their events at a local high school. Almost one hundred kids—bullied, bullies, and bystanders—were in attendance. The day starts with games, then connects kids through team-building activities and culminates in small groups where students open up and share their honest feelings. I was a small group leader. Powerful stuff.

"We've done it for several years now," Doug said. "And it's working!"

Is Point Break the key to the school's success?

I love Point Break, but honestly, it's just one of many practices Doug and his team are doing right. It's good leadership all around. Even the decision to have all his students attend an event like Point Break. It shows the school values kids' mental health as much as their education.

"Who am I to select which kids need an event like that?" Doug said.

Apparently the positive leadership is contagious. The school recently put on an orientation welcoming fifth graders who are slotted to attend the school as sixth graders next fall. Doug's middle school students shared testimony and performed skits providing incoming students with a peek at what they can expect at the school. Fifth graders left delighted, eagerly anticipating the start of classes at such a welcoming place.

If you walk on the campus, the adult presence is noticeable.

"Hey Jackson, Andrew, Daniel. . ."

Teachers and staff know every kid's name.

If you visited the school, you'd probably move into the neighborhood and sign up your kids in a heartbeat.

Is the school bully-free?

It's not incident-free. Just yesterday Doug told me a girl filled out one of the school's "Can we talk?" slips and reported a situation where one student intimidated another in the bathroom. Yes, actual paper slips that can be turned in unnoticed at a disclosed location in the office. Doug gets about fifty of them a month. They range from "Can I get a schedule change?" to "Mia wants to fight me." The simple communication tool helps Doug and his team deal with drama before it gets out of control.

And it rarely does.

I contrast this approach to what I've observed at so many other schools. Like one school where the principal roamed the halls as the archetypal disciplinarian.

"No running!"

"You!" He didn't know the boy's name. "Get your feet off that bench."

If a student approaches this principal and says, "I need to talk," the principal says (I kid you not), "You've got thirty seconds. Go."

While the kid talks, the principal simply stares at him for thirty seconds and then says, "Time's up."

And that's it.

These are the schools that have countless reports of bullying. Kids are left to fend for themselves.

Where are kids supposed to go for help if teachers and administrators aren't approachable?

Doug's school is getting an app next year. His teen daughter uses it at her school down the hill. The app allows you to pay for meals, access the school calendar, or use an anonymous tip line. Doug clicked on the tip line while we talked and read me the categories, listed in this order:

- Bullying
- Drugs
- Feedback
- Fighting
- Kudos
- Personal crisis
- Safety threat
- Vandalism

"We'll roll that out next year," Doug said.

So what's the secret to making a school a safe place for learning and growing?

Here are seven common denominators I've noticed in schools that seem to make their hallways and locker rooms safer places.

That's a good place to start: hallways and locker rooms.

1. HAVE A PRESENCE IN HALLWAYS AND LOCKER ROOMS.

The National Center for Education Statistics conducted a study of literally millions of kids across the US asking them if they were bullied, by whom, where, at what time, whether they used weapons. . .everything you can think of. This detailed study revealed the following locations as the places where most of the bullying occurred.

Among students who reported being bullied, the bullying occurred:

42%	Hallway or stairwell
34%	Classroom
22%	Cafeteria
19%	Outside on school grounds

| 10% | School bus |
| 9% | Bathroom/locker room[2] |

I have to admit, I was surprised to find only 9 percent had reported the bathroom or locker room. Again, we all see through our own lens, and I feared for my life while "dressing down" for gym class.

As I think back to the various accounts of bullying I heard, however, many of which I've shared in this book, I realize that most of them actually took place in the classroom or outside. And as I skim through my interviews, I see that the top four locations in the above study are probably the most common I heard.

Bottom line: Schools need to make sure they have a strong adult presence, especially in these locations.

I remember one of my bus drivers wearing headphones back when I rode the bus. Seriously, I'm not talking about Otto on *The Simpsons*. Kids said whatever they wanted on this bus. The driver might as well have had "privacy glass" between him and all of us.

We've all heard schools report they are making great strides to prevent bullying. Like what? Purchasing "Bully-Free Zone" posters?

Save your money and focus your attention on providing a positive adult presence around the campus. And I mean "around the campus."

One time when I was picking up my kids from middle school, I noticed close to seventy kids congregating in a field outside the school. I picked up my kids there every day, and there were never even ten kids in this field.

The two teachers standing out by the front parking lot were so engrossed in conversation with each other, they didn't even notice seventy kids in a field!

I got out of my car and went over there to see what was happening. It was a fight. One kid was on top of another giving him a severe beating. I broke it up and the crowd started jeering and calling me names I won't repeat.

Why were these middle school kids brave enough to start yelling at a random adult?

Because no one in authority was there.

So I whipped out my cell phone and started taking video of the crowd.

They dispersed immediately.

And the two adults never came over.

Come on, schools! *Really?*

One of the school counselors I interviewed told me about a young girl she counseled, a new kid at her school. At her last school she was targeted by a group of girls who said, "We're going to get you after school." She and her friend told some teachers, who advised, "Well, make sure you avoid those girls."

This girl was jumped and beaten to the ground after school while a crowd of kids gathered around and cheered. No adults were there. No one stepped in. The girl eventually switched schools.

Earlier in the book I mentioned a young man who has a huge birthmark on his face. As a kid he was publicly ridiculed on the playground. As he got older he got connected on social media to a whole group of kids with birthmarks to support each other. One kid had a birthmark over his entire eye. Kids called him "Sh*t Stain."

How do teachers and yard duty workers miss a bunch of kids calling another kid "Sh*t Stain"? Are you honestly going to tell me that no one's ears perked when they heard that nickname?

We need an increased presence in all these locations. I encourage schools to take a peek at the list on pages 166-167 and ask themselves, "Are we doing all we can to put a positive adult presence in these areas?" If you don't have the budget to hire more "yard duty," can you have a meeting with teachers and see if more teachers would be willing to keep their eyes open in these key areas? What about volunteers?

Don't just hire someone who is going to stand there and stare at their phone cluelessly while a crowd of kids around the corner surround a kid and beat him senseless. Which brings me to my second recommendation. . .

2. REPLACE CHAPERONES WITH SHEPHERDS.

We don't need chaperones who are simply punching a time card. We should look for shepherds who know kids' names and care about them.

> WE DON'T NEED CHAPERONES WHO ARE SIMPLY PUNCHING A TIME CARD. WE SHOULD LOOK FOR SHEPHERDS WHO KNOW KIDS' NAMES AND CARE ABOUT THEM.

Shepherds keep their eyes and ears open. They can spot warning signs if a kid is in distress.

One of the moms I interviewed had a son named Gabe who lost a finger at a young age. During kindergarten Gabe talked about the accident once at show-and-tell and it went pretty well. Kids asked questions.

"Does it hurt?"

"Do you still have the finger in a box or something?"

Addressing the issue seemed to help the situation.

In first grade Gabe did the same thing and it went well again. But in second grade. . .not so much.

Some of the kids told their older brothers and sisters, so older kids began to run up to Gabe on the playground. "Are you the kid with the freaky hand? Let me see it!"

"Gross!"

Crowds of kids would run up to him and stare at his hand, then run away, yelling, "Ewwww! Don't touch me with that hand!"

Again I ask, how do we *not* notice a crowd of kids running up to a kid with a known handicap and making a huge spectacle?

Where can we find caring adults who know what to look for?

When I worked for an organization called Campus Life, I used to go to the administration of local schools and offer to help in any way I could. Some schools gladly accepted our help. Other schools simply replied, "No thanks. We can't, since you're a pastor. You know, that church and state thing."

I knew the rules. I never "proselytized" on campus (that's literally what they called it if you talked about God). I was just a caring adult who talked with kids. But some schools were scared to bring in local youth pastors or volunteers from churches.

Until a tragedy hit.

Whenever there was a suicide or an outbreak of violence, all of a sudden we would get a call. "Can you guys come and be a presence on campus?"

After about a decade in the community, we built such a solid relationship with schools, respecting their rules and serving them with no strings attached, they let us come on campus anytime.

This was such a smart move for local schools. They had free help—and not just any adults but actual trained youth workers who loved kids and had their best interests in mind. Not chaperones with headphones.

Whoever schools recruit, they need to train them. They need to educate them on what to look for in potential bullies. Help them understand the difference between bullies, the bullied, and bystanders. Help them understand that bullies can be very smooth socially and the "favorites" of adults, whereas bullied kids are often shy or even awkward or difficult.

Do your adults know this?

Do your adults know not to rush to blame but to listen empathetically (everything we talked about in chapters 5 and 6)?

Yet adults aren't the only ones schools can mobilize to make a difference. Fellow students can make a huge impact.

3. INITIATE PEER COUNSELING.

Years ago, my sister-in-law Amy, the speech therapist, was teaching a class of first-, second-, and third-grade students in the Sacramento area. The students ranged in abilities, some with difficulties in reading, some with autism, some with behavioral issues and challenges. All of these kids had been bullied at some point in school.

One of the things Amy chose to do was to encourage students who had been suspended for bullying to become a regular part of her classroom during their recess times. Since they weren't able to handle recesses and were just sitting up in the office, they were assigned roles as helpers in Amy's classroom during their recesses. Amy trained these "bullies" to coach struggling readers, play games with students with behavior challenges, model good behavior in skits and role plays, and serve the students by handing out hand sanitizer and snacks.

But perhaps one of the most significant things she did was to refer to them as "leaders." She told them either they could lead people in the wrong direction or they could choose to lead people in the right direction. Either way, they were leading. But she emphasized to these "bullies" that leading in the right direction led to much happier and more fulfilling outcomes.

These initial "bullies" later that year formed a "bully patrol" on the playground and would assist yard duties by modeling good behavior at recess, encouraging kindness, and discouraging bullying. They even formed a bus patrol.

This group participated in weekly meetings (facilitated by Amy) to discuss how things were going on the playground and the bus, things that were working, and strategies they were going to try the next time.

Many of these students ended up spending most of their recesses helping out in Amy's classroom. It was a win/win. The bullies became positive leaders, special-needs students weren't being bullied and were actually developing friends and role models to look up to, and Amy got some extra classroom help.

My friend Kim started a peer counseling group at her school where kids could volunteer to help their peers and younger students in a variety of ways. One way they could help was by actually sitting with kids during lunch—not just once but for weeks at a time as part of the mentor program. These peer counselors were assigned which kids to hang out with, but most of the school didn't know who was assigned. They just saw two kids eating lunch together.

These kids actually received volunteer hours for the community service hours they needed to graduate.

Another part of the program was providing mentors for underclassmen. So a junior or senior would become a peer counselor for a freshman, spending an allotted number of hours together on and off campus during a given year.

Kim said the program was a wild success and created a wonderfully positive vibe on campus.

Do you offer leadership programs or "incentives" for kids to stand up and do something to combat bullying?

What about one-day events to address these issues? Let's take a peek at what these could look like.

4. GO BEYOND A TYPICAL ASSEMBLY.

I speak at school assemblies every year. I'll tell my story, encourage students that they can make a difference, and then give them practical tools to stop bullying before it starts.

But then I leave.

Do kids actually try out what I suggested at lunch that day?

Does anyone follow up on the practices I suggested?

School assemblies are great, but sometimes they lack follow-through and opportunity for students to practice skills that will help them apply what they learned and experience the feeling of making an impact.

Earlier in the chapter I mentioned a program in my city run by Youth for Christ called Point Break. Point Break is truly more than an assembly. It's an interactive day where kids talk through feelings, share insecurities, and identify with others who are experiencing the same things. They hear several talks from speakers, then dialogue about what they just heard in small groups, sharing their personal experiences and struggles.

The day ends with a powerful activity called "cross the line." One of the speakers who has spent the day with the kids reads questions and asks everyone to "cross the line" if they identify with that question. Small group leaders participated in this activity too. I crossed the line countless times.

Here are some of the questions they read to us that day:

- If you, as the speaker mentioned, often wear a mask rather than being your true self, please cross the line.
- If you feel like you have been challenged to be more encouraging with your words, please cross the line.
- If you have ever been teased or "trash-talked" on Snap, Insta, Twitter, Ask.fm, etc., please cross the line.
- If you have ever witnessed bullying or harassment on any of these social media platforms, please cross the line.
- If you feel like technology, being online, video

games, etc., has had a negative impact on your relationships, please cross the line.

- If you feel like no one understands you or listens to you, please cross the line.
- If you have ever been mocked, made fun of, or abused because of your race, culture, or heritage, please cross the line.
- If a family member or close friend has cancer or is dying, please cross the line.
- If you come from a family where alcohol or drugs are a problem, please cross the line.
- If your parents are divorced or currently separated, please cross the line.
- If you have ever witnessed domestic violence or been the victim of domestic violence, please cross the line.
- If you have ever had one or more family members in prison, please cross the line.
- If you come from a situation at home in which you feel like you have to be the parent, please cross the line.

For Girls Only. . .
- If you have ever felt like you were treated as less important than a guy, please cross the line.
- If you have ever thought you were not pretty enough, please cross the line.
- If you have ever felt like you were judged by other girls on campus, please cross the line.
- If you have ever been called a derogatory name by a man, such as slut, whore, or b*tch, please cross the line.

For Guys Only. . .
- If you have ever been told not to cry, please cross the line.
- If you have ever been hit to make you stop crying,

please cross the line.

- If you have ever been called weak, wimp, gay, queer, fag, or any other derogatory label, please cross the line.
- If you have ever been called one of these derogatory names by a family member, please cross the line.
- If you have ever felt like you needed to do something violent or dangerous to prove that you were tough, please cross the line.

After the workshop all the small group leaders fill out a form about their experience and then comment about each kid in their group, marking if there was a noticed need to follow up with kids urgently. School counselors eventually followed up with all the kids about the day, but some kids were marked as needing to be met with "within the week" and others "within twenty-four hours" because of something shared.

The Point Break workshop I attended actually launched an on-campus Campus Life club beginning the following week. Campus Life leaders acted as small-group leaders at the

AND THAT'S THE KEY. FOLLOW-UP.

Point Break event and then bridged that connection to the weekly on-campus program. The school loved this because Campus Life adult leaders helped them with the follow-up.

And that's the key.

Follow-up.

I've heard countless speakers talk about bullying, and I've heard great feedback from schools that have brought in guys like Nick Vujicic to talk about breaking barriers and pressing forward when others try to pull you down. I'm an advocate of these types of assemblies, but would recommend someone adding a "small group" component to follow. Effective speakers should be able to provide small group discussion questions for kids to digest what they've talked about. (I provide these all the time for groups when I speak to students.) This way we aren't just talking *to* students but also talking *with* students about what they're going through.

The more you dialogue with students, the more you can. . .

5. KEEP YOUR THUMB ON THE PULSE OF CONNECTION.

The most common cry I hear from lonely and dejected kids is "notice me." If kids feel isolated and unnoticed, often they'll turn to negative behaviors to get noticed. This is true for bullies and the bullied.

How can we prevent this?

Connection.

Again, one friend makes a difference.

The question is, do teachers and administrators actually know who has friends. . .and who doesn't?

We need to keep our thumbs on the pulse of connection in our classrooms.

Who's connected, and who's not?

Who is surrounded by their peers on the playground, and who's moping around by themselves?

Who had friends last week, but not this week?

In my research I came across a teacher who uses a fascinating technique to keep her thumb on the pulse of connection and disconnection in her classroom. Each Friday she has each of her students pull out a piece of paper and write down the name of four students they'd like to sit with the next week. She also has them nominate a student "whom they believe has been an exceptional classroom citizen that week." She collects all the ballots, places them in front of her, and looks for patterns:

- Who is not getting requested by anyone else?
- Who doesn't even know whom to request?
- Who never gets noticed enough to be nominated?
- Who had a million friends last week and none this week?[3]

No, she's not just rearranging her seating chart or looking for someone to award. She's "looking for lonely children."[4]

How many of your kids are feeling alone and isolated?

We need to have systems in place that help us identify kids who are constantly sitting or playing by themselves. Caring adults and peer counselors should start with these kids in their random acts of kindness or efforts to make kids feel noticed.

But connection also helps us keep a listening ear for reports of bullying. Which brings me to the next practice I believe schools should adopt.

6. GET ALL HANDS ON DECK.

We've read far too many stories in these pages where a victim of bullying heard the words, "Oh, just ignore it," or "They don't mean it."

Who determines which acts are "reportable" and which aren't?

Teachers and counselors know that certain words mean "mandatory reporting"—for example, if we hear a kid mention abuse, or the intent to harm themselves or someone else. By law we can't tell kids, "Your uncle didn't mean to do that. Just ignore him."

At the same time, we all know that sometimes kids have made these kinds of serious claims just for attention. I once counseled a young man who was so desperate for attention that he would start talking about cutting himself or being abused by a family member, claims that were both false. But as many times as he lied about these issues (and it was almost every time we talked), I didn't begin ignoring kids whenever they made these claims.

Schools need to put policies in place that take bullying claims seriously.

Some administrations are going to think this is nothing but "unnecessary paperwork." I know, because the state of New Jersey did exactly what I'm suggesting, passing a bill known as the Antibullying Bill of Rights. This legislation demanded "all public schools adopt comprehensive antibullying policies, increase staff training, and adhere to tight deadlines for reporting episodes."

When New Jersey did this, schools immediately contested, claiming they didn't have the time or resources to do this.

I agree.

Yes, I think you can't pass a bill like this without *also* providing funding to make it happen. Without the funding, schools will simply deem school guidance counselors and social workers as the new antibullying specialists. That's what happened in New Jersey, and schools complained they didn't have "the time or experience to look into every complaint of harassment or intimidation and write the detailed reports required."

IT SHOULDN'T TAKE A SCHOOL SHOOTING TO GET EVERYONE LISTENING.

I'm not a fan of red tape. I don't merely want to create paperwork.

I just want kids to stop hearing, "Ignore them and they'll ignore you."

We need to start taking these claims seriously. Schools can use apps or "Can we talk?" slips, whatever it takes to open the doors of dialogue about this important issue and to ensure that bullying claims are taken seriously.

It shouldn't take a school shooting to get everyone listening.

7. USE POSITIVE REINFORCEMENT.

One of my readers told me about an awards assembly at his son's school where teachers give out awards when they "catch" kids displaying antibullying behaviors.

"They make a bigger deal out of these awards than academic awards," he said. "We were shocked."

He described the awards ceremony.

> My eldest son received one of these awards. He came home one day with a slip of paper that told us we needed to attend an assembly the following week—he was going to receive an award. We showed up for the assembly, and after each class handed out their monthly academic awards, the principal came up and said she had a couple special awards to hand out. They were called Husky Hero

awards (our school's mascot is a Husky). For each award she handed out, she told why the student was receiving that particular award. My son had seen a girl sitting on the playground by herself. He walked over to her and asked her if she wanted to play with him. Another student saw this and let a teacher know that my son had done this. I was in tears as the principal told the story. Afterward, I asked him if he knew that girl or if he was thinking about earning an award when he helped her. He said he didn't know who she was and that he wasn't thinking about the award at all. He just saw someone that seemed alone, and he asked her to come play with him. As a parent, this award mattered more to me than any academic award he would ever receive.

Positive reinforcement is incredibly effective. I say it in almost every parent workshop I teach: "Catch your kids doing something right." If they do their homework without asking, tell them how proud you are. If they actually put their clothes in the laundry basket, not on the floor, then praise them! This kind of constructive feedback will make them want to repeat good behaviors.

Schools should look for every opportunity to reward good behaviors.

All good behaviors.

A youth pastor I know who works in urban ministry shared how he regularly will do a "starting lineup" introduction with a human tunnel, announcing the recent achievements that students have made. It doesn't matter if they got a small part in the school play, passed a class, or even got their GED. He makes an effort to find achievements kids have made and to praise them for a job well done.

The more we model this kind of praise, the easier it will be for kids to mimic it. If we model "dissing" and "teasing," they'll mimic those behaviors just the same.

DISCUSSION QUESTIONS

1. What was one thing in this chapter that really stood out to you?

2. What is one practice your school/your kids' school does really well?

3. What is one practice your school/your kids' school does that needs work?

4. Which of the seven common denominators Jonathan mentioned do you think is the most helpful? Why?

5. How can schools replace chaperones with shepherds?

6. What would it take to create a "peers helping peers" program at your kids' school? How could you help?

7. What is one specific thing you can do this week to help your school? What's the first step?

CONCLUSION
"THANKS FOR HELPING MY SON"

I can't possibly put into words how painful it is to watch your own child experience the torment of being teased and targeted. Many of you have firsthand experience with this. You know my pain. Nothing tears my heart more than seeing a young person ostracized and alone.

But it doesn't have to be that way.

I've seen parents, schools, and especially young people make a huge difference.

How?

By doing exactly what I've shared throughout the pages of this book: *noticing*, *listening*, *befriending*, and *empathizing*—and these are most impactful when done by another student. How many times have I repeated it: one kid can make a *huge* difference.

Cameron did.

Cameron is eighteen, a soccer player with blond-haired, blue-eyed good looks. Whenever you see Cameron at school, he's usually in the middle of a crowd. Cameron is never short a prom date, and he never eats lunch alone.

But like many young people Cameron's age, Cameron wanted to do something meaningful.

My friend Brian, a school counselor, encouraged Cameron to sign up for the "peers helping peers" program at his school. Cameron gave it a try, and that's where he was introduced to Jacob.

Jacob is a sophomore with hearing problems that hinder his speech, which has never helped his popularity. As if that weren't enough, he's on the spectrum.

Jacob ate lunch alone almost every day.

Until this year.

My friend Brian noticed Jacob's isolation. He didn't seem targeted or teased. . . just alone. But alone is never good. So Brian talked with Cameron.

"I think I've found just the kid for you to mentor."

"Really? Who?"

"His name is Jacob."

The two were introduced and ate lunch together.

"What do you think?" my friend Brian asked Jacob.

"He's nice."

Cameron agreed that Jacob would be a great kid to get to know. So the two began meeting.

Now, if you happened to be in the lunchroom on the tree-lined campus in Virginia, you'd probably see the two eating together every Tuesday. You might even hear Jacob laughing at Cameron's lame jokes.

Jacob's dad called the school and talked to my friend Brian.

"I don't know how to thank you."

"For what?" Brian asked.

"For helping my son find his smile."

Cameron broke through.

You can too.

Who is the kid on your mind as you read this?

What's one thing you can do right now to make him or her feel noticed and heard?

NOTES

Introduction
1. Jonathan McKee, "Three Ingredients Catalyzing the Spike in Teen Depression," The Source for Parents, October 31, 2017, http://www.thesource4parents.com/ParentingHelp/parenting-helpdetail.aspx?ID=148.

Chapter 1: View from the Edge
1. Quoted in Tammy B. Pham, Lana E. Schapiro, Majnu John, and Andrew Adesman, "Weapon Carrying among Victims of Bullying," *Pediatrics* 140, no. 6 (December 2017), http://pediatrics.aappublications.org/content/pediatrics/140/6/e20170353.full.pdf.
2. Sharon Jayson, "Bullying Survey: Most Teens Have Hit Someone Out of Anger," *USA TODAY*, October 26, 2010, https://usatoday30.usatoday.com/yourlife/parenting-family/teen-ya/2010-10-26-bullyingONLINE26_ST_N.htm.
3. Valerie A. Earnshaw, Marc N. Elliott, Sari L. Reisner, et al., "Peer Victimization, Depressive Symptoms, and Substance Use: A Longitudinal Analysis," *Pediatrics* 139, no. 36 (June 2017), http://pediatrics.aappublications.org/content/139/6/e20163426.
4. Christina Fisher, "The Association of Different Types of Bullying with the Mental Health of Children and Teens from the United States, France, and Canada," *Media and Communication Studies Summer Fellows*, paper 4 (July 24, 2015), http://digitalcommons.ursinus.edu/cgi/viewcontent.cgi?article=1003&context=media_com_sum.

Chapter 2: Just Ignore It
1. Mark Cendrowski, dir., *Big Bang Theory*. Season 11, episode 2, "The Retraction Reaction." Aired October 2, 2017, on CBS. https://www.cbs.com/shows/big_bang_theory/.
2. Julie K. Brown, "To Longtime Friend, School Shooter Nikolas

Cruz Was Lonely, Volatile, Ostracized," *Miami Herald*, February 17, 2018, http://www.miamiherald.com/news/local/community/broward/article200754714.html.

Chapter 3: Digital Hurt

1. Sy Mukherjee, "Study: Kids Who Are Cyberbullied Are Three Times More Likely to Contemplate Suicide," ThinkProgress, March 11, 2014, https://thinkprogress.org/study-kids-who-are-cyberbullied-are-3-times-more-likely-to-contemplate-suicide-5d929f7188c3/.

2. "What Is Cyberbullying?" Common Sense Media, accessed June 24, 2018, https://www.commonsensemedia.org/cyberbullying/what-is-cyberbullying.

3. "Complete History of Social Media: Then and Now," Small Business Trends, May 8, 2013, https://smallbiztrends.com/2013/05/the-complete-history-of-social-media-infographic.html.

4. "Teachers Charged with Computer-Related Crimes," *Tampa Bay Newspapers*, December 28, 2005. http://www.tbnweekly.com/pinellas_county/two-pinellas-teachers-charged-with-computer-related-crimes/article_5a8a6e34-258a-531b-ae60-56ef895d523d.html.

5. Jonathan McKee, "A Window into the MySpace Generation," The Source for Youth Ministry, February 14, 2006, http://www.thesource4ym.com/youthculturewindow/article.aspx?ID=122.

6. Wikipedia, s.v. "History of Facebook," last modified May 29, 2018, https://en.wikipedia.org/wiki/History_of_Facebook#cite_note-29.

7. Ruth McCormick, "Watch Steve Jobs Introduce the iPhone 10 Years Ago Today," The Verge, January 29, 2017, https://www.theverge.com/2017/1/9/14208974/iphone-announcement-10-year-anniversary-steve-jobs.

8. Charles Arthur, "The History of Smartphones: Timeline," *The Guardian*, January 24, 2012, https://www.theguardian.com/technology/2012/jan/24/smartphones-timeline.

9. Amanda Lenhart, "Teens, Smartphones and Texting," Pew Research Center, March 19, 2012, http://www.pewinternet.org/2012/03/19/teens-smartphones-texting/.

10. "73% of Teens Have Access to a Smartphone; 15% Have Only a Basic Phone," Pew Research Center, April 8, 2015, http://www .pewinternet.org/2015/04/09/teens-social-media-technolo gy-2015/pi_2015-04-09_teensandtech_06/.

11. Jay Donovan, "The Average Age for a Child Getting Their First Smartphone Is Now 10.3 Years," TechCrunch, May 19, 2016, https://techcrunch.com/2016/05/19/the-average-age-for-a-child-getting-their-first-smartphone-is-now-10-3-years/.

12. Monica Anderson and JingJing Jiang, "Teens, Social Media & Technology 2018," *Pew Research Center*, May 31, 2018, www.pewinternet.org/2018/05/31/teens-social-media-technology-2018/.

13. Marlow Stern, "The Nine Greatest Rap Disses: Kendrick Lamar, Jay Z, 2Pac and More," *Daily Beast*, August 14, 2013, https:// www.thedailybeast.com/the-9-greatest-rap-disses-kendrick-la-mar-jay-z-2pac-and-more.

14. Caroline Knorr, "Apps Stirring Up Trouble in Schools," Common Sense Media, September 25, 2017, https://www.common-sensemedia.org/blog/apps-stirring-up-trouble-in-schools.

15. Leora Tanenbaum, "What Teen Sexting Reveals about Women and Sexual Coercion," *Time*, January 18, 2018, http://time .com/5108384/teen-sexting-slut-shaming-me-too/.

16. Sara E. Thomas, " 'What Should I Do?': Young Women's Reported Dilemmas with Nude Photographs," *Sexual Research and Social Policy* 15, no. 2 (June 2018): 192–207, https://link.spring-er.com/article/10.1007/s13178-017-0310-0.

17. Saqib Shah, "UK Teens Say Instagram Is the Worst App for Cyberbullying," Engadget, July 20, 2017, https://www.engadget .com/2017/07/20/instagram-cyberbullying-survey/.

18. Suzanne Yeo and Catherine Thorbecke, "What Parents Should Know about the 'Constant Pressure' of Social Media for Teens," ABC News, November 21, 2017, http://abcnews.go.com/ Health/parents-constant-pressure-social-media-teens/sto-ry?id=50822684.

19. Adam Peck, "Victim's House Burned Down after She Accuses Football Star of Rape," ThinkProgress, October 14, 2013, https://thinkprogress.org/victims-house-burned-down-after-

she-accuses-football-star-of-rape-a8e5c995d1eb/.

20. Tara Culp-Ressler, "Cyberbullying Drove the Maryville Rape Victim to Attempt Suicide This Weekend," ThinkProgress, January 7, 2014, https://thinkprogress.org/cyberbullying-drove-the-maryville-rape-victim-to-attempt-suicide-this-weekend-8171f68f2b3a/.

Chapter 4: The Escape Key

1. Samantha Schmidt, "After Months of Bullying, Her Parents Say, a 12-Year-Old New Jersey Girl Killed Herself. They Blame the School," *Washington Post*, August 4, 2017, https://www.washingtonpost.com/news/morning-mix/wp/2017/08/02/after-months-of-bullying-a-12-year-old-new-jersey-girl-killed-herself-her-parents-blame-the-school/?utm_term=.16bb94245588.

2. Justin Zaremba, "Mallory Grossman's Parents Want Bullies Held Accountable in Daughter's Suicide," NJ.com, October 5, 2017, http://www.nj.com/morris/index.ssf/2017/10/parents_of_nj_girl_who_committed_suicide_take_to_m.html.

3. Victoria Ward, "Children Are Using Social Media after Midnight Every Day, Report Finds Amid Warnings Over Cyber Bullying," *The Telegraph*, February 26, 2018, https://www.telegraph.co.uk/news/2018/02/26/children-using-social-media-midnight-every-day-report-finds/.

4. Nitasha Tiku, "Health Experts Ask Facebook to Shut Down Messenger Kids," *Wired*, January 30, 2018, https://www.wired.com/story/health-experts-ask-facebook-to-shut-down-messenger-kids/.

5. Jean Twenge, "Teenage Depression and Suicide Are Way Up—and So Is Smartphone Use," *Washington Post*, November 19, 2017, https://www.washingtonpost.com/national/health-science/teenage-depression-and-suicide-are-way-up-and-so-is-smartphone-use/2017/11/17/624641ea-ca13-11e7-8321-481fd63f174d_story.html?utm_term=.045cda9b167c.

6. Brian X. Chen, "What's the Right Age for a Child to Get a Smartphone?" *New York Times*, July 20, 2016, https://www.nytimes.com/2016/07/21/technology/personaltech/whats-the-right-age-to-give-a-child-a-smartphone.html.

7. Melanie Curtin, "This Is the 'Safest' Age to Give Your Child a Smartphone, according to Bill Gates," *Inc.*, May 10, 2017, https://www.inc.com/melanie-curtin/bill-gates-says-this-is-the-safest-age-to-give-a-child-a-smartphone.html.

8. Katherine Hobson, "No Snapchat in the Bedroom? An Online Tool to Manage Kids' Media Use," Shots: Health News from NPR, October 21, 3016, https://www.npr.org/sections/health-shots/2016/10/21/498706789/no-snapchat-in-the-bedroom-an-online-tool-to-manage-kids-media-use.

9. Quoted in Susan Scutti, "Cell Phones and Screens Are Keeping Your Kid Awake," CNN, November 1, 2016, https://www.cnn.com/2016/10/31/health/kids-sleep-screens-tech/index.html.

10. Quoted in Amy Green, "Should Bedrooms Be No-Phone Zones for Teens?" *Psychology Today*, February 17, 2017, https://www.cnn.com/2016/10/31/health/kids-sleep-screens-tech/index.html.

11. "1 in 10 Visitors to Graphic Porn Sites Are under 10 Years Old," Fight the New Drug, October 23, 1017, https://fightthenewdrug.org/data-says-one-in-10-visitors-to-porn-sites-are-under-10-years-old/.

12. Jonathan McKee, "The Limp Truth about Porn," Jonathan's Resources, April 18, 2016, http://www.jonathanmckeewrites.com/archive/2016/04/18/limp-truth-porn.aspx.

13. Twenge, "Teenage Depression and Suicide Are Way Up."

Chapter 5: "Why Didn't You Say Anything?"

1. "Student Reports of Bullying: Results from the 2015 School Crime Supplement to the National Crime Victimization Survey," National Center for Education Statistics, December 2016, https://nces.ed.gov/pubs2017/2017015.pdf.

2. *Bully*, directed by Lee Hirsch (New York: Weinstein Company, 2012), DVD.

Chapter 7: The Bully

1. Alfiee Breland-Noble and Stacy Kaiser, "After School: Bullying," *Undercover High* Resources, accessed June 24, 2018, http://www.aetv.com/shows/undercover-high/season-1/episode-5

/after-school-bullying?playlist_slug=after-school.

2. Breland-Noble and Kaiser, "After School: Bullying."

3. "Butler Students Charged in Pineapple Assault," *Butler Eagle*, January 24, 2018, http://www.butlereagle.com /article/20180124/NEWS12/180129967.

4. "Three Teens Charged with Intentionally Exposing Fellow Student to Pineapple Despite Allergy," *Pittsburgh Post-Gazette*, January 26, 2018, http://www.post-gazette.com/local/ north/2018/01/26/teens-charged-pineapple-allergy-exposed-fellow-student/stories/201801260114.

5. Rachael Pells, "School Cyberbullies More Likely to Attempt Suicide, Study Finds," *Independent*, August 16, 2017, https://www .independent.co.uk/news/education/education-news/school-cy-berbullies-attempt-suicide-thoughts-kill-themselves-study-so-cial-media-messages-a7895731.html.

6. Matt Gutman and Josh Haskell, "Rebecca Sedwick Suicide: Parents of Alleged Cyberbully Blame Facebook Hack," ABC News, October 16, 2013, http://abcnews.go.com/US/parents-alleged-rebec-ca-sedwick-cyberbully-blame-facebook-hack/story?id=20583537.

Chapter 8: The Bystander

1. "Time with Tunes: How Technology Is Driving Music Consumption," Nielsen, November 2, 2017, http://www.nielsen .com/us/en/insights/news/2017/time-with-tunes-how-technol-ogy-is-driving-music-consumption.html.

2. Roni Caryn Rabin, "Reading, Writing, 'Rithmetic, and Relationships," *New York Times*, December 20, 2010, https://well.blogs .nytimes.com/2010/12/20/reading-writing-rithmetic-and-rela-tionships/.

3. Craig Brandhorst, "Adolescent Bully and Peer Intervention," Phys.org, March 2, 2017, https://phys.org/news/2017-03-ado-lescent-bully-peer-intervention.html.

4. *Hotel Rwanda*, directed by Terry George (United Artists and Lionsgate, 2004), DVD.

Chapter 9: The Bullied

1. Ryan Smith, Ashley Louszko, John Kapetaneas, and Lauren Ef-

fron, "When the Pain, Torment of Cyberbullying Lingers Years Later," ABC News, March 24, 2015, http://abcnews.go.com/Health/pain-torment-cyberbullying-lingers-years/story?id=29867617.

2. Smith, Louszko, Kapetaneas, and Effron, "When the Pain, Torment."

3. Smith, Louszko, Kapetaneas, and Effron, "When the Pain, Torment."

4. Benoit Denizet-Lewis, "Why Are More American Teenagers Than Ever Suffering from Severe Anxiety?" *New York Times Magazine*, October 11, 2017, https://www.nytimes.com/2017/10/11/magazine/why-are-more-american-teenagers-than-ever-suffering-from-severe-anxiety.html.

Chapter 10: Real-World Solutions

1. "Depression and Anxiety: Exercise Eases Symptoms," Mayo Clinic, September 27, 2017, https://www.mayoclinic.org/diseases-conditions/depression/in-depth/depression-and-exercise/art-20046495.

2. "15-Year-Old's 'ReThink' App Aims to Prevent Cyberbullying," Yahoo! News, August 26, 2015, https://www.yahoo.com/gma/15-olds-rethink-app-aims-prevent-cyberbullying-142145500--abc-news-BackToSchool.html.

3. Jonathan McKee, "Gunning Your Kids Down," Jonathan's Resources, February 26, 2018, http://www.jonathanmckeewrites.com/archive/2018/02/26/gunning-your-kids-down.aspx.

Chapter 12: School Shootings

1. Snejana Farberov and Louise Boyle, " 'He Called Him a Rat Face': Classmate Reveals Suspect, 16, Who Injured 21 in School Stabbing Spree Was Bullied on Facebook the Night before Bloody Rampage," *Daily Mail*, April 12, 2014, http://www.dailymail.co.uk/news/article-2603009/Alex-Hribals-classmate-reveals-suspect-16-injured-21-school-stabbing-spree-BULLIED-Facebook-night-bloody-rampage.html.

2. Rich Cholodofsky, "Alex Hribal Gets Up to 60 Years in Prison for Franklin Regional Attack; Bullying Claim Denied,"

TribLive, January 22, 2018, http://triblive.com/local/westmoreland/13191726-74/alex-hribal-gets-up-to-60-years-in-prison-for-franklin-regional.

3. Lorraine Adams and Dale Russakoff, "Dissecting Columbine's Cult of the Athlete," *Washington Post*, June 12, 1999, http://www.washingtonpost.com/wp-srv/national/daily/june99/columbine12.htm.

4. Andrew Blankstein and Corky Siemaszko, "Washington School Shooting Suspect Wanted to Teach Bullies a 'Lesson,'" NBC News, September 24, 2017, https://www.nbcnews.com/news/us-news/washington-school-shooting-suspect-wanted-teach-bullies-lesson-n801346.

5. Rachel Alexander and Eli Francovich, "Bullying Too Simple an Explanation for Freeman School Shooting, Experts Say," *Spokesman-Review*, September 17, 2017, http://www.spokesman.com/stories/2017/sep/15/bullying-too-simple-an-explanation-for-freeman-sch/.

6. Adams and Russakoff, "Dissecting Columbine's Cult of the Athlete."

7. Augusto S. De Venanzi. "School Shootings in the USA: Popular Culture as Risk, Teen Marginality, and Violence against Peers." *Crime, Media, Culture.* 2012.

8. Pham, Schapiro, John, and Adesman, "Weapon Carrying among Victims of Bullying."

9. Blankstein and Siemaszko, "Washington School Shooting Suspect Wanted to Teach Bullies a 'Lesson.'"

Chapter 13: Locker Rooms and Hallways

1. To learn more about the Point Break program, visit www.pointbreakonline.com.

2. "Student Reports of Bullying: Results from the 2015 School Crime Supplement to the National Crime Victimization Survey," National Center for Education Statistics, December 2016, https://nces.ed.gov/pubs2017/2017015.pdf.

3. Glennon Doyle, "Share This with All the Schools, Please," Momastery, January 30, 2014, http://momastery.com/blog/2014/01/30/share-schools/.

4. Doyle, "Share This."

MORE GUIDANCE FOR PARENTS & TEENS!

The Teen's Guide to Social Media and Mobile Devices
by Jonathan McKee

McKee shares helpful tips for today's teens and tweens navigating the digital world. With tips like *Nothing you post is temporary* and *Don't post pics you wouldn't want Grandma, your boss, and Jesus seeing! (Jesus is on Insta, you know!)*, Jonathan's approach is refreshingly honest and humorous, as one who knows teens and understands the way they think. He provides information for them to make informed decisions and challenges them in a way that encourages and inspires—without belittling.

Paperback / 978-1-68322-319-1 / $12.99

The Guy's Guide to God, Girls, and the Phone in Your Pocket
by Jonathan McKee

The Guy's Guide melds spiritual and practical advice with humor—a winning combination for teens trying to navigate the ups and downs of real-life with confidence and wisdom. Guys will be encouraged and challenged with sound, biblically-based advice equipping them to live the Christian walk every day—while encountering some humorous, common-sense tips along the way.

Paperback / 978-1-62416-990-8 / $12.99

For more resources about bullying prevention or to bring Jonathan to your city to speak go to
BULLYINGBREAKTHROUGH.COM